Paying
the
Piper

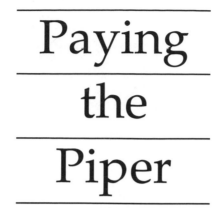

Paying
the
Piper

Culture, Music and Money

ALAN PEACOCK

EDINBURGH UNIVERSITY PRESS

THIS BOOK IS DEDICATED
TO THE MEMORY OF
HANS GAL

© Alan Peacock, 1993

Edinburgh University Press Ltd
22 George Square, Edinburgh

Typeset in Adobe Palatino
by Æsthetex Ltd, Edinburgh,
and printed in Great Britain by
The University Press, Cambridge

A CIP record for this book is
available from the British Library.

ISBN 0 7486 0458 8
ISBN 0 7486 0454 5 (paper)

CONTENTS

ACKNOWLEDGMENTS

I am grateful to the editors of the following journals and newspaper for allowing me to reproduce passages from my own articles:

The Three Banks Review (later *Royal Bank of Scotland Review*)
The Musical Times
The Times

The passage from Hans Gal's *The Musician's World* quoted in Chapter 1 is reproduced with the kind permission of his publishers, Thames and Hudson, London.

PREFACE

When I left what would surely be my final assignment as Homo Quango – Chairman of the Scottish Arts Council and a member of the Arts Council of Great Britain (1986–92) – I thought it a good moment to set down a few ideas about the political economy of the arts. An easy way of doing this would have been to assemble an edition of collected articles and papers written over the last twenty-five years. I have gone through this type of operation before, but have not found it an entirely satisfying experience. Edinburgh University Press were prepared to proceed on these lines, and I contemplated writing the usual apologetic introduction justifying the selection and claiming that I had a few fresh thoughts to offer in some supplementary notes. However, its Chairman, David Martin, made it clear that he would still prefer a new book, reminding me of his amusing aside some years ago that he was always surprised at how well my books for him had sold! Flattery, even of this qualified kind, will get him anywhere, so I have obliged him, though I have inserted one or two excerpts from previous publications where it seemed appropriate. Besides, most of the articles would have had to be addressed to those with a knowledge of economics, or at least of the economist's ways of thinking, and I agreed with EUP that perhaps it was time an economist justified to a wider public the contribution of his/her subject to understanding the world of culture.

I thought for a long while and decided that I could avoid some of the more austere features of the professional discourse of the economist if I offered a memoir of my close encounters with the world of the arts. If greater accessibility was a cardinal consideration in my mind, the decision to write about my personal life was not an easy one to make. One may get carried away by the belief that one's autobiographical reminiscences are both interesting and important. David Hume warned us that 'it is difficult for a man to speak long of himself without vanity' and reduced his autobiography to ten pages. The personal details I have given are only those which I felt were necessary to understand what led me to take a particular view on such matters as the economic position of the composer and on funding the arts. After Chapter 1 I say little about my personal life and professional career as an economist, and that is probably just as well.

My publishers requested me to range far and wide over the arts as I have been closely concerned for a concentrated period with Arts Councils' policies covering creative and performing arts, together with public service broadcasting. I have accommodated them by having a fair amount to say about the political economy of the arts in general, sufficient, I believe, to justify the sub-title of the book. However, my comparative advantage in economic investigation of the problems of culture lies principally in the field of music. As I reveal in Chapter 1, I was once tempted to believe that I might make a stab at becoming a composer. My passage towards involvement with policies for the arts brought me mainly into contact with the musical profession, as later chapters make clear, but much of what I have to say in them, particularly in the two final chapters, considers matters pertinent to the creative and performing arts as a whole.

Many of those to whom I owe a particular debt of gratitude are mentioned in the text but I must add to that list the names of several friends and colleagues who have helped me in various ways. First of all, amongst professional economists I must include Hilda and William Baumol and Mark Blaug, colleagues and friends for many years. Bruno Frey, Werner Pommerehne, Gianfranco Mossetto, David Throsby, Michele Trimarchi and Ruth Towse, all now members of Centro Internazionale di Studi sull'Economia dell'Arte of Venice, have raised issues which I might not otherwise have considered. During my Arts Council days, it was rare to have a Minister for Arts and Libraries as receptive to new ideas as Richard Luce, now, by a curious coincidence, my lineal successor as Vice-Chancellor of the University of Buckingham. My predecessor as Chairman of the Scottish Arts Council (SAC), Gerald Elliot, has for several years conducted a dialogue with me on practical questions of arts funding which have given me much to ponder over. The two Vice-Chairmen who had to suffer me, James Logan and Brian Ivory, will recognize certain incidents in my narrative recalling occasions when they restrained me from completely casting aside the normal codes of gentlemanly conduct; and they are both admirable persons with whom to hold a friendly debate. Seona Reid, successor to Tim Mason (see Chapter 7) as Director of the SAC, will long remember, I hope, moments when she wondered whether all economists were quite as mad as she regarded me; but she was the soul of tolerance, as were all my fellow members of the SAC during my period of office. Mrs Eva Fox-Gal kindly gave me additional information about her father's life and work. I must also thank Dr David Smith, Director of the Borthwick Institute of Historical Research at the University of York, who facilitated access to the archives of the Orchestral Employers' Association which enabled me to cross-check my account of the events described in Chapter 4. Finally, the process of production has rested on the support of The David Hume Institute which has meant, as on many past occasions, relying on Kathy Mountain to deliver clean copy with her usual commendable speed and accuracy.

1

TUNING UP
Don't Put Your Son On The Platform, Mrs Peacock

Life can be regarded as a series of episodes in which our illusions about our ability to achieve the targets we have set ourselves are frequently destroyed. The process of meeting self-appointed challenges and experiencing failure by one's own standards does not necessarily make one unhappy and bitter. Nor if one is old and is occasionally asked for advice does it lead one to advise the young to be hesitant and cautious so as not to risk the failures that one has oneself experienced.

All my life – indeed up to the moment of writing this book – I have wanted to be a professional musician, and a composer in particular. I shall never be more than a competent player, if that. Margaret, my wife, answers enquiries about my musical abilities by saying that I can play any tune at sight on several instruments – badly. That is an exaggeration of my talents. I shall never be able to write music of any profundity employing vast orchestral and vocal forces. My lessons in composition taught me at least what I did not know. But this does not make me unhappy or discontented. My musical education, much of it self-education, has greatly enhanced my appreciation of music itself, which is not to argue that being knowledgeable about music is a necessary condition for enjoying it. My family know that music fulfils an important emotional need, and they are on their guard – and out of sight – when some personal upset drives me to improvise at the piano.

But the reason I mention and elaborate on my musical interests now is that my unwillingness to give up my aspirations entirely has brought me into continuing contact with professional players and composers whom I have learnt to admire greatly, not only as individuals but as a profession. It was probably inevitable that at some stage in my professional career as an economist I would find myself investigating the economic circumstances governing their activities and how they reacted to it. An obvious choice for research work on completing my undergraduate studies would have been a study of the supply of and demand for musical services. In retrospect, I am glad that I never even considered the matter. I would have had to train myself in asking the right questions and in a field of economic enquiry which hardly existed. 'Cultural economics' only received professional recognition as a category of economic enquiry in 1992, when the American Economic Association added it to its Classification of Economic Disciplines. Enthusiasm for music might have coloured my judgment of musicians' behaviour in the market place, probably losing the respect both of those whom I wished to study and certainly of those who had to judge my professional work.

BEGINNINGS

I suppose that there was nothing atypical in my musical education in a city, Dundee, far removed from London when the metropolis was increasing its vice-like grip on our musical life, even more in the early 1930s than hitherto, through the development of broadcasting. My parents bought an upright Steinway in the late twenties, the first piece of family furniture bought on the instalment plan, raising the eyebrows of relations who always paid on the nail for everything except a house bought on mortgage. A Miss Cordiner taught my sister Joan and me piano, but, more important, she taught me how to read music, through the very effective device of sharp and painful blows on the knuckles with a pencil when there was a disparity between her expectation of my performance and the sordid reality of my response. I could sing quite well and had an excellent music teacher at the local elementary school who had seven-year-olds singing parts of Schubert's 'Schöne Müllerin'. Subsequent lessons on the violin and viola confirmed that I would never be anything more than an indifferent executant, though I rationalise my poor showing by the fact that I started string-playing at the late age of eleven. (I now play viola in a practice orchestra and, after a fifty-year gap, am actually taking viola lessons from a stern young lady who believes that there are vestiges of technique remaining in my aged fingers.)

I faced an unexpected problem with my teachers and fellow pupils. The development of my tastes and musical interests far exceeded that of my playing technique. In those days, even internationally known musicians made extensive provincial tours in celebrity concert series, and in the Caird Hall, Dundee, I heard Fritz Kreisler twice – nestling his head in the chin rest of his violin as if contentedly asleep. To have heard this fine musician, who was a composition student of Bruckner, and then, not long afterwards, Frederic Lamond, advertised as Liszt's last pupil, appeared to me as an astonishing link with a very distant past; but then, some years later I was taught composition by someone who had seen Gustav Mahler conduct. There was, too, the Scottish Orchestra led for a short time by that wonderful violinist Henry Temianka and conducted successively by Barbirolli, Szell and Susskind. Szell could produce a galvanising effect at times. He was not above venting his wrath in public on the horn-players, which should have detracted from but, for me, added to the attraction of the performance. When would he explode next?

My exposure to a wide range of music was not confined to the war-horses of the repertoire. Dundee High School employed a most unusual Head English Master, Mr Borland, who gave the impression of being the typical Scots dominie yet was passionately devoted to the sharing of his obsessional interest in music with the rest of the Upper School. He extracted money from the school to pay really outstanding chamber ensembles on tour to perform on the afternoon of their evening public performance. I suspect that he got a cut rate from their agents, as the school concert could be treated as rehearsal time – one of my first lessons in the finance of music. He insisted that the honour of the school was at stake unless a large and 'attentive' audience were to be present and this meant that two or three times a year he sent out a three-line whip which was extended to the school staff. Who of my generation, outside those with close connections with the music profession and living in London, could have heard, and in my case deeply enjoyed, not only the standard quartet repertoire of Haydn, Mozart, Beethoven and Schubert but also

Debussy (still then regarded as deliciously decadent), Fauré, Ravel, Bloch, and even Charles Ives, Elliott Carter and Samuel Barber? My wife, who was actually a pupil at St Paul's Girls' School when Holst, Vaughan Williams and Herbert Howells formed the magnificent succession of music masters, cannot recall that any similar opportunity was open, at least to those who were not being individually taught.

One night in the mid-thirties, I passed the house of the new incumbent of St Luke's Church, Broughty Ferry, and was deeply impressed by the splendid piano-playing. I was too shy to call, but I resolved to contrive to get to know Tom Keir and his wife, Ivy, who sang beautifully. Many Scots should be grateful to him for his revision of the Hymnary of the Church of Scotland, which displays his formidable knowledge of contemporary music, as well as his reverence for the finest kind of Christian religious music. They gave me a wonderful welcome and offered probably my first experience of being treated as an equal in any discussion – a sure way to make one acutely aware of one's shortcomings while encouraging one to overcome them. Over fifty years later, a visit to him always leaves me with some new thing to ponder over after he has drawn my attention to some striking musical passage that he has rediscovered or has played something of his own, perhaps a finely crafted hymnal setting. It was Tom who introduced me to Bach, but also to much modern piano music, then almost unavailable on records.

While there are huge omissions from this list of twentieth-century composers – I did not hear Schoenberg's *Verklärte Nacht* until 1946 – their work had hardly penetrated the teaching repertoire. It was not unnatural, I suppose, that I became regarded as a musical snob, and my violin and piano teachers, who had probably little desire or much opportunity to treat listening to modern music as a relaxation, made the most of pointing out to me that I had better learn to play the easier classical repertoire properly before moving on to the fancy stuff. They were probably right, and my obstinate unwillingness to undergo hard training tortured by the scales of Clementi, Czerny and Kreutzer put paid to any possibility that I might get professionally involved with music. The door finally closed, as I realised many years later in examining the data presented in Chapter 3, when it became obvious to me that the last thing I wanted to do was to become like my teachers – yet music teaching is the mainstay of professional composers.

It was galling, nevertheless, for a musical snob to be relegated to the role of third violin in a three-violin arrangement of selections from *Il Trovatore* in the annual concert of Miss Robertson's string pupils. Worse still was to see the honours being taken by a short, fat Italo-Scot with an ingratiating smile, who brought the house down – encore insisted upon – with a gooey but technically impeccable rendering of Toselli's *Serenata* – that magnificent late Victorian tear-jerker.

If I could not play sufficiently well for others to enjoy or be impressed by my technique, I could have a stab at writing music and my first composition, a Prelude allegedly of the Debussyesque genre, was written when I was about thirteen. Pages and pages were to follow, and I even persuaded two sisters who played violin and cello to join me as the viola player in a String Trio written in their honour. It was tuneful enough but a second performance was studiously avoided. I tried to differentiate my product by writing under the assumed names of Anatol Pavlin and Vladimir Kressel and the girls' mother gave me some visiting cards inscribed with the latter name as a humorous birthday present. By this time, when I was about fifteen plus, my parents, who had paid little attention to my educational progress at school, suddenly woke up to the fact that I had personally arranged to drop Mathematics from my preparations for the School Leaving Certificate, and had substituted Lower Music which, as it did not involve more than a simple knowledge of pianistic technique, could be passed without difficulty by someone who could already read a score, knew all the Beethoven symphonies and could tell a triad from a tritone. My father got the blame for this, but acceded to my request that his colleague Harry Willsher, the Librarian of University College, Dundee, and a musicologist, should have a look at my compositions. My hopes that he would recommend that I became a composer were blighted. He recognised a certain melodic gift but nothing more and, as well as pointing out the uncertainties and consequential dangers of a musical career, rightly emphasised that only the very few could live by composition alone and technical musical skills of a high order were a precondition for even modest success. It was good advice which was hard to take. I did pass

Lower Music and had a most agreeable oral examination with
David Stephen, then a well known Scots composer, who was
illustrating Harry Willsher's point by having to supplement his
earnings by examining spotty teenagers like myself. My covert
substitution of music for mathematics meant that my Leaving
Certificate did not accord with university entrance qualifications
and the subsequent retrieval of my academic fortunes meant
concentrating on the hard struggle of making up lost ground.
The outbreak of the Second World War in any case postponed
any thought of becoming a votary of St Cecilia.

WAR AND MUSICAL EXPERIENCES

A great deal has been written about the influence of war on the
arts. I am not thinking so much of the inspirational effect on
composers and the opportunity it gives for programme music
in which battles rage and heroes fall – there was plenty of that to
come, particularly from Russian composers inspired by the *1812*
tradition. More relevant in my own case as with so many music
lovers was the therapeutic effect of playing and listening when
life was difficult, at times dangerous, and relaxation severely
restricted. For most of us of military age, we could no longer
expect to enter a trade or profession, if jobs would have been
available, finding ourselves replicating the lives of our parents,
although they, too, had been through the trauma of the 1914–18
war and felt lucky to have survived it. We were to be faced
with compulsory military service uprooting us and planting
us in unfamiliar places, along with others with vastly different
backgrounds, tastes and preferences. Forgetting my two years
at the University of St. Andrews, where I sang in the choir,
wrote a viola sonata, and began to play quite respectably on the
recorder, three and a half years in the Royal Navy took me to
such diverse locations as 'Pompey' (Portsmouth) and Devonport
Barracks, Sheerness (which seemed the end of the world), courses
on Naval Intelligence work in Wimbledon, Cheadle (Staffs),
Newbold Revel, Southwick in order to equip me for sea time
in the North Sea, the English Channel, and the Arctic on the
Russian convoys, and ending up as the Assistant Prize Officer
in Kiel, Germany, where I had to formally receive the surrender
of German naval and merchant craft when hostilities ceased. (I
also got married to Margaret and we had started a family just

as I returned to university to finish an honours degree – but that is another story.)

This variety of naval experience was accompanied by what must have been unusual opportunities to develop musical interests, as compared with what otherwise might have happened. As Margaret was a WRNS officer in London, even limited leave periods offered opportunities to attend concerts at the Albert Hall and the famous series at the National Gallery. The Naval Intelligence service, 'Y' branch, seemed to be full of musicians of various degrees of proficiency. If I once knew Mozart's 'Linz' and 'Haffner' symphonies note for note, it is because Jack Davies and I spent hours at Scapa Flow playing a four-handed version for piano whilst waiting for the next trip to maraud shipping on the Norwegian coast. If I smile every time I hear Beethoven's 'Spring' Sonata for violin and piano, it is because Victor Kanter dragged his violin around the Home Fleet and in a rough sea off Jan Mayen Island I accompanied him on a ship's harmonium found in the storeroom of an Escort Carrier. If I am haunted by Anton Rubinstein's 'Rolling Waves', it is because I heard it sung so beautifully by a young Russian bass, Mischa Riba, in the hangar of HMS *Victorious* anchored in the Kola inlet after avoiding a U-boat attack and ploughing through mountainous seas. Mischa was a member of a concert party sent to entertain us. The ordinary matelots thought they would witness the Russian equivalent of a seaside pierrot show, but were astonished to find that they were to listen to a string quartet and two singers. Most of them had never heard classical music before and that ship's company was one of the most well conducted and appreciative audiences I have ever encountered. It was thirty years before I heard 'Rolling Waves' again, by the chance buying of a record of Russian romantic songs sung by Kim Borg. We did not quite manage to find enough players to form an orchestra at Kiel, but I did play clarinet in a small dance band specialising in South American music.

I met several professional musicians and a composer or two during the war. They unfortunately confirmed the previous warning that you had to be pretty tough and hardbaked to survive orchestral life and there was no expectation that things would improve whatever promises of a New World might be offered by a grateful government when hostilities ceased. It was a shock to find that such a fine keyboard player as Walter Bergmann, who also had much to do with the revival of baroque music during and after the war, served behind the counter of Schott's music shop in Marlborough Street, W1. Clutching my copy of Paul Hindemith's *Traditional Harmony*, which I think I bought there, I must have seemed the epitome of artlessness.

On one occasion I arrived at Schott's with a neatly written manuscript of a small choral piece by a forty-six-year-old German 'sailor' drafted into the German Navy during the last months of the war. The 'sailor', who was assigned to me as an orderly of some kind, turned out to be the Professor of Composition at the Staatliche Hochschule at Graz. He offered me some lessons and I embarked on an extremely austere examination of *cantus firmus*, possibly the result of his having examined my copy of Hindemith's *Traditional Harmony*, and finding it full of pedagogic short-cuts which worried him considerably. I was to discover that he was a well known choral composer who had studied with Carl Orff, and was all the more mystified that he insisted on such a strict regimen. This was my first direct encounter with the extreme thoroughness of Germanic musical training. It must not be forgotten how strict Arnold Schoenberg was in such matters. It is an open question whether I would have survived his course, though he was the most charming and considerate of teachers, which was not simply a reflection of my having managed to reduce his official duties to a minimum. I was not tested because I was demobbed not very long afterwards. The only service I was able to render him was to dispatch a large quantity of manuscript paper to him at a time when it was impossible to find in occupied Germany. He merits an entry in *The New Grove Dictionary of Music and Musicians*. To those who associate me with the Scots tradition of political economy, it will appear ironic that his name was – Karl Marx.

THE LURE OF LONDON

After nearly three years in St Andrews completing my degree and subsequently lecturing in Economics there, I was persuaded by Margaret to apply for a Lectureship at the LSE. To our surprise, the application was successful. The domestic and intellectual upheaval are only marginally relevant. I only mention that a surprising number of my colleagues at St Andrews viewed the LSE with intense suspicion and the Professor of Divinity, meeting me in College Street in the academic jewel of the north, announced for all around to hear that 'LSE's an awfie wicked place'. (As recently as February 1993, the same view was expressed to me by Sir Denis Thatcher!) For a young ex-serviceman this only whetted the appetite, though I suspected that, with Lionel Robbins, Friedrich von Hayek and James Meade as my senior colleagues, I would be in the midst of the most respectable academic company. Tempted though I am I must not digress on the influence they and others exercised on me. I owe an enormous amount to them which I hope I have adequately acknowledged elsewhere.

The enormous advantages of London as a musical centre easily induce a passive approach to their enjoyment, and not only because of the immense variety and easy accessibility of musical events, for Covent Garden and the Festival Hall were within easy reach, and the old Stoll Theatre, which occasionally had touring opera, was only round the corner. A more important influence which could have engulfed me was the intensity with which a fair proportion of my LSE colleagues followed cultural events and felt impelled, almost obliged, to comment on them. A good part of Senior Common Room conversation between its older members would have been impossible to understand without the acquisition of at least a superficial knowledge of the standard dramatic, orchestral and operatic repertoire but also of the professional virtues and vices of the artists who presented these cultural gifts to the metropolitan audience. It was not merely a question of knowing your Shaw or your Verdi but also of being able to follow the discourse on the virtues of X's compared to Y's interpretation of some dramatic or vocal masterpiece. I suspect that in the cut and thrust of discussion of 'le dernier cri' in art, music, drama and literature there was a bogus element, and provocative and clever remarks were made as much to turn the conversation into a battle of wits with which to entertain an admiring audience, at the cost of any serious assessment of the artistic events that the participants had been lucky enough to see and hear.

I certainly do not mean to disparage this intense concern with being *au fait* with the latest artistic development though I still remain sceptical of artistic judgments made by those who are purely observers, however sensitive and imaginative, without having themselves tried their hand as creative writers or composers or as performers. Some of my senior colleagues were certainly closely engaged with the world of culture as trustees of galleries and artistic companies and readily shared their knowledge of professional opinions on what to see and hear. This was a useful point of departure for younger colleagues who would otherwise not know where to begin to allocate what small amounts they could afford to spend on visiting exhibitions, concert halls and theatres. Then, too, there were colleagues who were remarkably proficient as writers and musicians. Amongst my senior colleagues, Henry Phelps Brown, outstanding labour economist and economic historian, gave a graphic account of the retreat to Dunkirk in his novel, *The Balloon*, published by Macmillan, and based on experiences still fresh in the minds of all ex-servicemen. James Meade, later Nobel prizewinner in Economics, sang lieder with a beautiful high baritone voice and ran a madrigal group which he asked me to join. Tom Marshall, the sociologist, knew more about music than anyone and played beautifully on the viola. Amongst my contemporaries, Claus Moser, later to be the Chairman of the Governors of Covent Garden, made me realise what a bad pianist I was, and now has an outstanding reputation as a musician as well as a statistician. Donald Watt, international historian, was a most versatile operatic baritone, who had sung major roles with the Oxford Musical Society. Michael Wise, later one of the country's best known geographers, was a most proficient accompanist with catholic tastes. If Lionel Robbins was not himself a performer or composer, one always felt that he could have emulated us all, had he set his mind to it. Along with Tom Marshall, and our Director, Alexander Carr-Saunders, he regarded artistic interests and pursuits as an integral part of the life of the school.

The absorption of cultural influences by some form of osmotic action would never have satisfied me, though the uncovenanted benefits received by listening to my colleagues' views on and experience of culture were immense. At the very least it reduced the 'search costs' of finding out what was going on and how it was viewed by both artists and audiences. My first attempts to become actively involved in music again were abortive. It was a mistake to try to play the viola again without lessons, which I could ill afford; and equally it was a mistake to take clarinet lessons when I was promoted to Reader and could just about afford them. However, as luck would have it, on an occasion when there was no clarinet part in a piece being tried out by the LSE orchestra, I was asked to stand in for the missing conductor, usually a music student at one of the London academies. I seemed to manage reasonably well and, no doubt because I would not expect or demand a fee, I was asked to conduct for the remainder of the academic session.

Being a conductor of a small amateur orchestra in a place of such intellectual sophistication as LSE offers a test of all-round musicianship. The potential audience, as I have indicated, would be knowledgeable and have critical standards, given the alternative availability of excellent professional performances. The 'resource inputs' in the form of students and staff willing to subject themselves to collegiate scrutiny would depend on the chance of student and staff recruitment based on their actual or potential competence as social scientists and not as musicians. Matching the repertoire to the quality and quantity of resources could be difficult and the orchestra and chorus themselves might view the 'job satisfaction' from the potential repertoire differently from the conductor. Once the repertoire was decided on and practices arranged, orchestral and vocal parts might require editing, and parts might have to be reassigned to 'fill in' for instruments for which no players could be found – cellos may be less difficult to come by than bassoons. Tempi and dynamics may not be clear in scores, and, even if they are, concessions may have to be made with difficult passages. A fair proportion of players may never have played in an orchestra before or have learnt to listen to each other – not that such a requirement is universally followed or even accepted by professionals! The act of co-ordination of sounds required of a conductor means developing a *rapprochement* between conductor and players unlikely to be perceived as necessary in a professional orchestra used to playing a large part of their repertoire almost in their sleep, and sometimes even looking as if they were. The large bulk of the work of a conductor, as is well known, is commonly all but complete before an actual concert takes place.

I have to remind myself that there has been an explosion in the amount of music available in both live and 'canned' form since those days in the 1950s. Therefore, it may surprise the reader to know that it was relatively easy to pick pieces of music or even operas which were never performed but which are now part of the standard repertoire. A concert version of *L'Elisir d'amore* which Donald Watt and I concocted with him singing, Michael Wise as continuo and myself conducting was regarded as a surprising and enjoyable novelty, though it would not have been possible without Donald's recruitment of excellent soloists, one of them, Doreen Murray, later singing principal roles at Sadler's Wells Opera. Somehow that year we had a very good crop of student singers and players for our chorus and orchestra. The main problem I encountered was finding orchestral parts which were tracked down to manuscript copies which the Librarian of Covent Garden kindly lent us. They had not been touched for over fifty years. The famous bassoon accompaniment to 'Una furtiva lagrima' had to be played on the cello, but this worked surprisingly well.

I well understand the temptation open to prima donnas whose memoirs turn into successive descriptions of their triumphs, but I must desist from further examples of our doings, even at the cost of leaving unmentioned other players and singers – several of them to become occupants of Chairs of Economics, Statistics and Economic History in different parts of the world – who joined our risky ventures. But I cannot miss out a splendid performance by Claus Moser of the Mozart Piano Concerto in A (K414) which began with Claus leaning over in my direction and whispering: 'meet you, Alan, at the double bar'.

My days as maestro were numbered for shortly afterwards I accepted a Chair at Edinburgh University. While the attractions of such a post were obvious to a thirty-three-year-old, how I could drag myself away from the metropolis was not easily explained to musical friends. Perhaps some instinct warned me against being drawn in to the maelstrom of London cultural life where it is difficult for the amateur not to conform to passing fashions and fancies. A lady colleague of mine at LSE put the metropolitan view very well by consoling me with the observation that 'after all, Edinburgh is one of *the* only *other* places'. She herself was a Scot who had long been de-tribalised.

HANS GAL

The purpose of this narrative being to establish what credentials I may have to explore the problems of cultural economics, I can pass by the very small part that I played in musical life when we moved to Edinburgh, though some elderly persons still seem to remember my playing buffo roles in *La Belle Hélène* and *Fra Diavolo*. Margaret worried slightly in case, after taking a few singing lessons, I might just be able to make the chorus of a third-rate opera company, and desert my Chair. A much more important experience concludes the 'praeludium' which is of particular relevance to what follows.

I first met Hans Gal through my dentist who was a member of the Edinburgh Musicians' Club. Hans Gal was giving the first performance of his own *24 Preludes* which I was astonished to learn he had written while stuck in a hospital bed. He must then have been seventy. I had only heard a few of his compositions on radio, but I was very taken both with the composer and with his latest creation. Clearly my assessment of his work would be worthless, but my impressions on that occasion are pithily expressed by Conrad Wilson who wrote of Gal's music that '[h]is musical roots lay in Brahms and Strauss and it was in the tonal tradition of those composers that he continued to work, pouring out a tireless flow of classically constructed, glowing-toned pieces, finely crafted, courteous, orderly, and unhurried in their musical discourse' (Wilson, 1980, p. 91). I was yet to experience what Wilson has called 'the vitality and perceptiveness of his musical opinions' (ibid.).

Shortly afterwards, I noticed an advertisement in *The Scotsman* in which Dr Gal intimated that he was willing to take private pupils in composition and pianoforte. With some trepidation I went to see him with three songs for baritone which I had written for Donald Watt and which we had perpetrated at some LSE concert. I imagine that he was more intrigued than impressed by one song, a setting written in the form of a polonaise of a poem called 'Tanz nach Art der Polen' by the German baroque poet Simon Dach. How come that an Economics Professor might know anything of German literature and have the temerity to tackle that most difficult of art-forms, the lied? Like Harry Willsher, he detected some melodic facility in my writing, and perhaps he liked the challenge of seeing what he could make of a younger colleague whose knowledge of music might make up for his technical incompetence. He took me on and changed my musical life. I am eternally grateful to him.

Hans Gal taught harmony and counterpoint to me entirely by example. He wrote music as one composes a letter, and if he wished to illustrate, say, fugal form, he would start to write a fugue and simultaneously explain what he was doing. Nothing could be more exhilarating than to see a piece written in front of one's eyes rather than to have to dig up examples from a textbook. If he felt it necessary to illustrate a point by reference to some composer or other, he would draw on his incredible memory, and sometimes just play the relevant passage through on the piano – he was, as is well known, an excellent pianist. I have watched him, breathless, while he transcribed at sight the full orchestral score of Max Reger's *Variations on a Theme of Heller* for piano, simply in order to explain how free variation form can be tackled. He was also not averse to showing how even great composers might have difficulties in resolving some problem, for, as he was fond of saying, 'there are three problems in writing music – how to begin, how to continue, and how to end'. His illustration about ending difficulties was to take three examples from Verdi operas! His small, spare figure would disappear up a ladder to pull out the scores, which he carefully replaced when he had completed his didactic demonstration. I never believed that he would have me writing a double fugue movement for a string quartet within a few months. My own progress is not of concern here, but the insight that I received into the composer's mind and methods helped me later to establish rapid rapport with musicians when circumstances demanded it.

I owe him much more than an addition to my musical under-standing. At the end of a lesson we would frequently converse about wider aspects of his profession. He made no secret of his passions and prejudices. When I remarked, rather jocularly, that I thought that the Reger variations were not likely to be established in the repertoire, he glared at me and said: 'Each country likes to be bored in its own particular way by its native composers. In my native Austria and in Germany, we had Max Reger; in France and

Belgium there is, of course, César Franck; and what do you have
in your country? Why, *all* the symphonies of Vaughan Williams!'
I tackled him on the Second Viennese School. He was amused by
the uncritical acceptance of the twelve-tone system as the only
mark of compositional progress. He told me that he had once
lectured in the USA on the School and had tested his audience
by playing six short pieces of his own composition, five of
which randomised the notes and the sixth of which was written
according to the strict Schoenbergian canon. His audience was
asked to identify the *echt-Schoenbergisch* but rarely did. But I was
wrong to charge him with arguing that no outstanding music was
being written other than in a post-Straussian style. If he had not
felt the need to follow the twelve-tone Piper of Vienna, he could
still admire the work of those who were lured into following him,
being himself a friend of Alban Berg. Rather to my surprise, he
expressed the greatest admiration for Prokofiev whom he rated
much more highly than Stravinksy. But I have also seen Hans
conduct a performance of great finesse of the latter's *Apollon
musagète*.

He paid me the compliment of taking economics seriously and
we would talk sometimes about economic and social questions,
though not frequently enough, I realise in retrospect, about the
economic problems of the arts. If we did, he never mentioned his
own bitter experiences of having to leave Austria and Germany
where his reputation was firmly established as a composer of
operas, some of which had been performed in major German
opera houses. It would be an impertinence of me to dwell on
these, and I mention them only because it made him acutely
aware of the hazards which inflicted so many of his profession.
Fortunately for the world at large, Hans Gal's biographies of
composers, while minor masterpieces of appraisal of the works
of Brahms, Schubert and Wagner, also show a remarkable insight
into the effect on them of their social and economic environment.
Fortunately for my own investigations, he published a wonderful
collection of composers' letters, interlaced with his own carefully
worded and penetrating observations. This collection is called
The Musician's World.

An excerpt from this work forms a useful 'bridge passage' to
the next part of my narrative. It is revealing because it shows both
the knowledge, perceptiveness and wit of the compiler and also

the appreciation by Verdi of the economic principle of 'marginal utility':

PROSPERO BERTANI TO VERDI

Reggio (Emilia), 7 May 1872

Much honoured Signor Verdi,

The 2nd of this month I went to Parma, drawn there by the sensation made by your opera *Aida*. So great was my curiosity, that half an hour before your commencement of the piece I was already in my place, No. 120. I admired the *mise en scène*, I heard with pleasure the excellent singers, and I did all in my power to let nothing escape me. At the end of the opera, I asked myself whether I was satisfied, and the answer was 'No'. I started back to Reggio and listened in the railway carriage to the opinions given upon *Aida*. Nearly all agreed in considering it a work of the first order.

I was then seized with the idea of hearing it again, and on the 4th I returned to Parma; I made unheard-of efforts to get a reserved seat; as the crowd was enormous, I was obliged to throw away five lire to witness the performance in any comfort.

I arrived at this decision about it: it is an opera in which there is absolutely nothing which causes any enthusiasm or excitement, and without the pomp of the spectacle, the public would not stand it to the end. When it has filled the house two or three times, it will be banished to the dust of the archives.

You can now, dear Signor Verdi, picture to yourself my regret at having spent on two occasions thirty-two lire; add to this the aggravating circumstance that I depend on my family, and that this money troubles my rest like a frightful spectre. I therefore frankly address myself to you, in order that you may send me the amount. The amount is as follows:

	Lire
Railroad – going	2.60
Railroad – returning	3.30
Theatre	8
Detestable supper at the station	2
	15.90
Twice	31.80

Hoping that you will deliver me from this embarrassment, I salute you from my heart.

Bertani

My address: Bertani Prospero, Via San Domenico, No. 5.

VERDI TO HIS PUBLISHERS, MESSRS RICORDI, MILAN,
ENCLOSING THE PRECEDING LETTER

[*May 1872*]

You may well imagine that to protect the son of a family from the spectres which pursue him, I will willingly pay the little bill which he sends me. I therefore beg you to forward by one of your correspondents to this M. Prospero Bertani, at Reggio, Via San Domenico No. 5, the sum of 27 lire 80 centimes. It is not the amount he demands; but that in addition I should be expected to pay for his supper, certainly not! He might very well take his meals at home.

It is understood that he will give you an acknowledgement, and further a short letter in reply, undertaking to hear my new operas no more, exposing himself no more to the menace of spectres, and sparing me further travelling expenses . . . .

RECEIPT

Reggio, 15 May 1872

I the undersigned acknowledge to have received from the maestro G. Verdi the sum of 27 lire 80 centesimi, by way of repayment of my travelling expenses to Parma to hear *Aida*, the master having considered it fair that this sum should be returned to me, as I did not find his opera to my taste. It is at the same time agreed that in future I shall not make any journey to hear new operas of the maestro unless I undertake the entire expense, whatever may be my opinion of his works.

In faith of which I have signed,

Bertani Prospero

Note the grounds on which Verdi rejected the claim for the 'detestable supper'. The petitioner would have had supper in any case, so this did not represent part of the loss of utility that he claimed to have suffered!

CODETTA

'Don't put your daughter on the stage, Mrs. Worthington' advised Noel Coward. 'Don't put your son on the platform, Mrs Peacock' was equally good advice. Yet I believe that knowing what happens on the platform and on the stage, while it risks engaging my sympathies with my subject matter and may therefore affect my objectivity, has the compensating advantage of affording a better appreciation of the aspirations, motives and actions of musicians faced with the binding economic constraints which affect us all.

2

PRELUDE
In the Beginning Was Wilfred

INTROIT

It was really all Wilfrid's doing, that is Wilfrid Mellers, Professor of Music at the University of York where I was his professorial Economics colleague. If you don't know about him, you should. In *The New Grove Dictionary of Music and Musicians*, he merits three and a half columns. In the final sentence of the entry which precedes an enormous list of his compositions and books about music, you read that in his latest work 'the diatonicism of his earliest style is still present but takes place in a more flexible sound spectrum that incorporates glissandos, clusters, indeterminately pitched and non-pitched sounds as well as controlled improvisation, all to some extent influenced by Mellers's interest in the recreation of natural, animal and primitive human sounds in a ritualized musical context'. Do not be put off by this kind of professional claptrap. Even if Wilfrid occupies twice as much in Grove as my mentor, Hans Gal, and excites the jealousy of those amazed at the adulation and attention showered on him by female students, he is a great figure in music. He has much not to be modest about.

Before I explain what Wilfrid asked me to do I have to offer a parallel explanation for the rather sniffy nature of this introduction. The idea of setting up a music department in the University of York can be fairly claimed by Philip Brockbank and myself, one of the few things on which we were not in profound disagreement. We sold it to the Vice-Chancellor, Eric James, and the only other two professors so far appointed in 1962,

Gerald Aylmer and Harry Ree. We would all make substantial sacrifices in staff and resources in order to cross-subsidise and so nurture this tender plant of Music. It was Philip's idea to appoint Wilfrid who had read both English and Music at Cambridge, an acceptably clever move which would bring Music into the pull of the Arts orbit.

One condition of his appointment was that he should find a place for the Granada Arts Fellow whom we had been able to fund through Eric James's power of painless extraction of money from Lord Bernstein. He was David Blake (also already a Grove-man though twenty-two years younger than Wilfrid). David won the famous Mendelssohn Prize awarded for study abroad. He told me that in making his choice, he examined the list of his forebears, most of whom had studied in Italy, and the only one for whom he had any respect was Arthur Sullivan. So he went to study with Hanns Eisler in East Berlin. We forget that the composer of the East German National Anthem was a pupil of the very stern teacher of traditional harmony, Arnold Schoenberg, and the thoroughness of Schoenberg/Eisler training shows up in David's work. (Sounds like more professional claptrap – apologies!) I confess to liking David's music more than Wilfrid's and almost as much as Hans Gal's and I also enjoy his deprecatory sense of humour. I remember him offering a pre-launch talk on his Violin Concerto at the Proms at which one member of the audience asked him why David, a Marxist, should have sold out to the establishment by being in post as a Professor instead of being at the cultural barricades. He replied: 'well, the money's good'.

You must have guessed what is coming. The tender plant of Music burgeoned. Music became the cult subject at York, with Wilfrid leading a dedicated regiment of (primarily) composers from behind, with occasional flamboyant excursions to the front of his troops. Students, cash and compliments flooded in and we were treated to splendid concerts from all manner of musicians for whom the York association had become important, and were allowed into the workshops of the avant-garde provided we were suitably respectful. The high point in the early days should have been the appointment of the Amadeus as the resident quartet, but the students, fired by the cult of modernism, understandably complained about the traditionality of their programmes. I recall remonstrating with Siggy Nissel of the Quartet that at one concert they had played some modern piece with markedly less enthusiasm than a Brahms quartet. He wryly remarked: 'Well, Alan, Brahms was really quite a good composer!'

In the heady days of the 1960s, when sociologists and Leavisites vied with one another to capture the high ground of cultural influence in universities, the centre of gravity in economics was moving away from university departments. The prevailing philosophy was that intense technical input into mathematical modelling and statistical verification would not only improve economic forecasting but make it possible for economic planners to improve the economy's growth prospects. Economists who followed the cult of technocracy have really only themselves to blame if they began to be regarded as committed only to the worship of Mammon; and there is a long tradition amongst economists that they practise the 'science of material welfare'. One of my tasks in this work will be to disabuse the reader of that idea. I shall argue that economics is not about how to increase the supply of material goods but is concerned with the analysis of human choices all of which require material inputs. That I did not succeed in convincing my colleagues in other disciplines of this point is to my detriment. More's the pity because I was persuaded to leave a Chair in Political Economy in ancient Edinburgh in order to set up the social sciences in new York by Lionel Robbins, the great protagonist of economics as the science of choice. Our local image at York was as conservative enemies of progress, judging society's improvement solely in terms of material success, based on a sordid view of human motivation. It was an easy if false step to imagine that we had no time for interest in, or commitment to cultural pursuits of a higher order. Our students risked being branded as the Calibans of the campus, enjoined to study with the purpose of training their eyes to seek out the main chance. It is not certain that this view was sincerely held by all those opposed to the growing pretensions of economics; but it was a convenient rationalisation for those who dramatised their position by the well tried technique of shouting 'those who are not with us are against us', much used, it must be noted, by disciples of Freud.

It probably did not help matters if the economists, along with a fair number of specialists in the natural sciences, just got on with the job and did not argue the toss about which discipline was head of the pile. In a subject where one was no longer judged by erudition but by one's analytical ability and practical skills much of the drudgery and pedantry of scholarship was cast aside. The interesting point here is that although there was no obvious way in which music and economics could be combined, York was developing a music department with a similar intellectual outlook. Original composition and new ideas on performance preceded musicology in the hierachy of preferences. The problem presented by economists, one supposes, is that they were completely sceptical of the pretensions of music and drama as instruments for social and economic change. For composers with a *verismo* streak in them the capitalist must always be a villain and the worker a hero. Nothing else makes artistic sense.

Now I can tell you what Wilfrid did and why it altered my life, a fact of which he is probably completely unaware. He knew that I had an interest in music. David Blake had tolerated my presence in the first University Orchestra concert in the last desk of the violas, because I had enough musical skill to know when *not* to play. I attended and discussed concerts. I showed Wilfrid two compositions. The March, he said, was pure Prokofiev, which, although dismissive, pleased me for it indicated that I had progressed beyond traditional harmony and counterpoint. The Passacaglia was not really a passacaglia at all. I had to return to the extensive underground of amateur composers – a fair judgment. But I had my uses, for I might be influential as Deputy Vice-Chancellor, and an economist might know something about musical patronage which was becoming an issue which no university department could afford to ignore. So I accepted with alacrity his invitation to address a conference of composers and impresarios on the economist's view on public patronage and music. The truth being told, I was rather flattered, and a little apprehensive. I really did want to put on a good show. I realised how much music meant to me and how, like a child, I craved the attention if not the admiration of its professionals. Simultaneously, I hoped that an economist might become regarded as almost human, though some of my professional economics colleagues regarded an attempt to apply economics to the arts as a sign of the early onset of senility.

In short, between the two of us there appeared to be mutual

gains from trade with low transaction costs – see, we economists are not to be left behind when it comes to clap-trap! Both of us were maximising utility under conditions of uncertainty, for Wilfrid did not know what I would come up with, and, I must confess, neither did I. What follows is a stripped down version of what I produced for his conference and my first entry into the then unknown subject of 'cultural economics' – about which much more will have to be said.

PUBLIC PATRONAGE AND MUSIC
(as it appeared in 1968)

Bernard Shaw (1955) (using the pseudonym of Corno di Bassetto) wrote some of the best musical criticism of the late nineteenth century, but was tempted to predict that economic growth tempered with social justice would be enough to ensure the commercial survival of serious music. The evidence collected by Professors Baumol and Bowen (1966) in their highly original study suggests that he has turned out to be wrong. Musical activity as measured by the number of live performances over the last twenty years has grown steadily, but the index in costs of performance has been rising at a faster rate than the index of receipts. Baumol and Bowen claim that the 'income gap' may widen even further in both the United Kingdom and the United States.

It seems odd that this should happen. True, as Baumol and Bowen put it, 'from an engineering point of view, live performance is technologically stagnant', so that the quartet Op. 59, No. 1 of Beethoven still requires the same labour input and playing time as it did in 1820. Therefore, substantial productivity gains have not compensated for the growth in the remuneration of musicians. Nevertheless, one might have expected that the growth in the incomes of those in the industries which have had substantial increases in productivity would have been reflected in an ever-increasing demand for the products of the service industries such as music. The likely explanation seems to be that the public's demand for music is being increasingly satisfied by the mass media of radio and television and the availability of an enormous range of recorded music at low prices. Besides, the 'on-costs' of attending a public performance – travel cost, meals and baby-sitter fees – are likely to be noticeably more than those incurred at home, even allowing for the capital costs or rental of stereo and television.

Accepting our authors' evidence must signify that if the community wants to see live performance of music and drama flourish, public patronage or encouragement of private patronage seems essential. Further, if cultural survival depends on encouragement to new or unfamiliar works, then the need for support is still more urgent.

In London, for example, 556 musical works were performed in the Festival Hall and Albert Hall combined between mid-September 1966 and mid-September 1967, of which 93 were by living composers but only a handful by composers under fifty, thus justifying the composer Arthur Honegger's (1966, p. 19) wry remark that 'it is clear that the first specification for a composer is to be dead'. Taking the UK as a whole, the balance of advantage for the dead is probably a good deal greater than for London alone.

The Musician's View

It seems natural to begin any investigation of the question of patronage by seeking the opinion of those who create and execute the works to be performed. As we shall see, even a sympathetic observer must be struck by the lack of sustained thinking by the music profession about the dilemma in which it finds itself.

The Youth Employment Service rightly warns aspirant composers in their 'Choosing a Profession' series of handbooks that composing rarely provides a living by itself, for it is well known that royalties from publication and fees for performance of works are relatively insignificant and irregular sources of income. Composers have come to terms with this situation in various ways. The Russians, Borodin and Cui, were respectively a professor of chemistry and an army general, while the now much-played American, Charles Ives, sold insurance. Debussy married a rich widow; Tchaikovsky and Wagner found rich patrons in Madame von Meck and Ludwig of Bavaria. Now that the technique of composition and knowledge of music generally are more exacting than hitherto and rich widows and other patrons have been crushed out of existence by inheritance taxation, composers tend to keep alive by sticking more closely to musical activities. Conducting, playing, editing and teaching music, or a combination of some or all of these jobs helps to keep the wolf from the door.

It is an interesting question what effect these various side activities have on the form, content and quality of music. In a fascinating essay the contemporary American composer, Virgil Thomson (1962) has claimed that one can predict the source of income from the style and choice of media of composers, but concludes that 'excellent music can be written on almost any kind of money'. Few outstanding composers who have voiced their feelings on the matter agree with him, the general claim being that the ideal situation is one in which the composer is left untroubled by the problem of making ends meet. Stravinsky (1962), for example, demands, quoting Ezra Pound, that the artist should be in a position where he 'can work as he likes or waste his time as he likes, never lacking provision', adding in his own words: 'That should be read by anyone who intends to commission an artist'.

In seeking to achieve this desired state of affairs, composers rarely offer practical advice. They treat with contempt any suggestion that composers are producing a product or service for others, although, as we shall see later, Paul Hindemith has some good advice to offer in this respect. Schoenberg (1965) speaking of the listener writes: 'all I know is that he exists, and in so far as he isn't "indispensable" for acoustic reasons (since music doesn't sound well in an empty hall), he is only a nuisance' – hardly a recipe for survival! Schoenberg's pupil, Hanns Eisler (1964), claimed that 'the present position of the modern composer is that of a parasite and sponger. The function of music in capitalist society is entertainment'. To Eisler, the only solution (which his teacher incidentally deplored) was not, as Michael Tippett (1959, p. 153) has suggested, for creative artists to 'bear their tribulation like a rose', but for them to throw in their lot with the agents of the class struggle – the proletariat – who in some inscrutable way would recognise the good composer for what he is worth. More plausible seems to be the conviction of Virgil Thomson (1962) that the composer should follow the executant in ensuring his rights by unionisation, adding 'the doctors have done it. So can we'. Executants, like doctors, it seems, have a much earthier view of their economic position, and their attempts, often highly successful, at 'work spreading' and employment creation are too well known to require further mention.

Even if one sympathises with the view that 'to him who hath talent shall be given and no questions asked', clearly it would have no influence in gaining public support and would offer little guidance as to how funds, inevitably limited by competing demands for resources, should be administered, far less as to how they are to be raised and from whom. For who is to decide who has talent and who has not? Judging by what musicians say about one another's music, one may be excused for being a little worried about the exercise of patronage by representatives of the patronised!

In sum, I doubt whether professional musicians and artists are the best people to plead their own case, at least in present circumstances, and what follows is an attempt to make it for them in, I hope, more realistic and acceptable terms.

The Case for Public Support

We live in a society which expresses its choices about the use of resources in two ways: through the market and through the ballot box. The case for expressing choices through the ballot box is usually made on the grounds that not all the community's needs can be achieved, even if they wanted them to be, by buying and selling. The implication of choice through the ballot box is that the funds to finance these community needs have to be provided by compulsory exactions: taxes. Therefore, the fundamental question is, why should society as a whole bear any part of the support costs of music? For a case to be made, it must be proved that there are benefits to the community at large over and above the benefits accruing to the relatively few who attend the performances.

A beginning can be made by asking the question, are there any special risks attached to music which might seriously affect the supply of musicians and thereby the future of the performances? So far as instrumentalists and singers are concerned, the evidence seems to suggest that relatively low and precarious earnings in relation to their training and education has not resulted in a drying up of the springs of talent, although avoiding action against poverty by executants who take on heavy work schedules may affect the quality of playing. So far as composers are concerned, there have always been problems associated with the protection of their intellectual property. It may be recalled that the only way of seeking to prevent piracy open to Beethoven was a public declaration in the Viennese press against the offending publishers, but today the laws of copyright provide at least adequate protection against unauthorised publication and performance in most parts of the world. In such circumstances, the financial risk to composers, impresarios and publishers are very much less than they would otherwise be, although their interests are not always identical.

In short, there does not appear to be any reason why music should be singled out for special treatment on grounds of risk in a society which at least accepts that full employment, adequate income support during unemployment and other social measures are there to protect the working population. The Goodman Committee (1965, p. 6) went so far as to suggest that subsidies to orchestras were open to abuse, adding that 'we cannot help feeling that in some cases concerts have been promoted without being justifiable on either commercial or artistic grounds, their main *raison d'etre* being to provide work for members of the orchestra'.

A second set of arguments is based on the proposition that the 'normal' economic model of a competitive economy ignores certain technical features of production which may make the market inefficient in achieving general objectives of policy. For example, official thinking on subsidising music is very much influenced by the argument that our great national artistic institutions should 'form, as it were, an international show-case' and that 'a country which is putting public money into a number of artistic enterprises wants a return from its spending in both national *and international* acclaim' (Higgins, 1965, p. 319). The only way to cater for a demand to improve our nation's cultural image is, at the very least, to underwrite the production of, say, new music which would not otherwise take place. Apart from the obvious difficulty of deciding how much international prestige is worth, the difficulty here is to establish that, pound for pound, public support for music offers more community satisfaction than, say, association football. Even if the present author woulds gladly record his vote for music, he must admit, reluctantly perhaps, that there is no *technical* economic argument allowing us to conclude that the views of a cultural minority should take precedence over those of others.

Let us take this argument a stage further. There may be cases in which a national or local community may benefit economically by offering musical performances at less than cost as a means of attracting visitors; what may be termed the 'balance of payments' argument. This is because music is a 'joint product' supplied together with accommodation, meals, even souvenirs, although itself the necessary (but not sufficient) condition for visitors coming at all. Receipts from visitors may be maximised by offering music as a 'loss leader' and subsidising performances from the receipts from, for example, those lines of production which benefit most from 'overseas trade'.

In an enlightened community, it is possible that voluntary cross-subsidisation of music by the beneficiaries might provide the necessary funds, but clearly the market provides no mechanism which would allow the sponsors of music to capture these benefits automatically. Consequently, it is argued, public finance, national or local, is necessary. It is to be noted once again that music is merely regarded as a means to an end – improvement of local incomes. What has to be proved is that music provides a *better means* of achieving this objective than others.

The arguments so far, and they seem far from conclusive, concentrate on the employment or production benefits of music, and therefore objectives which can be achieved by other and possibly more effective means at least in some instances. More conviction might attach to an argument which supported subsidies to music on grounds of its unique, direct benefits to the consumer as listener. One such argument is deployed by Baumol and Bowen which this author finds somewhat more persuasive than the others. To paraphrase their view: we are concerned about the judgment of posterity in our treatment of the development of culture, including music. Even if we may be individually sceptical of contemporary developments and are not prepared to pay directly for ordeal by contemporary music or drama, we may sanction public action, if need be by state support, to be sure that future generations have the chance of judging present-day developments for themselves. In the persuasive words of Baumol and Bowen (1966, p. 384), 'few of us are willing to take the responsibility of passing on to future generations a country whose beauty has been destroyed'. Therefore the state must intervene. Stravinsky may be right in saying that 'great, i.e. immortal, music creates its own need', but – let it be added – only after a time-lag.

There is, of course, no guarantee that future generations will approve of the legacy of culture provided by what support we afford music now, and it must be assumed in the argument that culture, once stunted or destroyed, could never be revived. However, what is important for the argument is the view taken *now* of future generations' needs, for by the time their views are known, we shall not be here!

The Extent and Form of Public Support

The Extent of Support

Nothing in what has been said so far gives us any clue as to the *amount* of support. All that can be offered in this connection is a warning against specious arguments about 'technical means' of determining the 'optimal' expenditure on music. No doubt one could quantify the financial support necessary for a given number of concerts per annum or for x number of commissions for compositions or for the running costs and capital costs of increased support for musical education. This might be a useful first stage in drawing up a 'music budget' for a Minister of State. In the end, however, whatever the level of government, such a budget has to be compared with other competing claims for funds, the 'cost' to the community of expenditure on music being measured, however approximately, in terms of the alternatives forgone: less for other arts, less for defence and so on.

The fact remains, nevertheless, that the ultimate decision rests upon a value judgment – the tastes and preferences of leg´ ators – and it would be foolish to rely upon 'blinding by science' as a method of influencing their opinions. It is a disagreeable facet of life that the arts will only prosper through public action when politicians need the cultural vote, or through the energy, enthusiasm and influence of politicians and senior administrators in positions of power.

The Form of Support

By the form of support we may mean either the alternative media of performance or the budgetary methods chosen to finance these media.

On the first of these forms of support, I have very little to say. Clearly the major problem in this connection is devising principles of allocation, once the total budget is known. The fundamental difficulty is one of aesthetic judgment. If we believe that we are the custodians of a cultural property to be bequeathed to our heirs, does it make any difference whether we put all our resources in national institutions such as Covent Garden Opera and the Royal Ballet or spread it more thinly over a vast array of orchestral and chamber concerts up and down the country? Even if one accepts the principle that only musicians should pass judgment on this matter (and this itself raises some further issues about the rights of consumers as well as producers), it is clear that they are unlikely to be unanimous in their opinions. As a liberal, my only solution is based on a belief that once state influence on the form of musical activity through the budget is granted, we should not encourage cultural monopolies. I am glad to accede to the view that the division of funds should be largely left to a panel of the musical profession, *provided that frequent changes are made in its membership*. Here we have a parallel case to the disbursement of funds for research by the state. Natural or social scientists are fully competent to decide whether or not particular research projects would be carried out in a scientific way, but are unlikely to be able to judge with any precision how these projects should be ranked in seeking to attain any particular objective, even one as superficially clear-cut as improving the rate of economic growth.

I suspect that it is even more difficult to rank musical projects according to their contribution to 'cultural advance'. Hence the recommendation that there should be a fairly quick turnover of membership of any committee doling out the lolly.

The second way of looking at the form of support is according to the financial method used. First of all, one can influence the extent of musical activity in specific directions by reducing its supply price. Probably most of us see this being done by a direct subsidy to the appropriate organisation supplying new musical performances so that it can either employ more resources than it would otherwise do at existing prices of admission or can reduce the prices of admission to concerts requiring no unusual input of resources. Either way, those who organise concerts must not be surprised if authorities disbursing the funds insist on some clear statement of the concert budget and some form of accountability, if only as a protection to the taxpayer who is footing the bill. Coming to terms with the harsh realities of financial control is something one has learned to live with in other areas relying on state support – in my own case economic research – and freedom in research is only achieved at the expense of time spent in careful explanation of its aims and objects. Perhaps the reason why the arts have fallen behind is not purely the prevalence of philistinism. As it has been put by the Rockefeller Panel Report on the Performing Arts (1965), 'Artists are frequently inarticulate in explaining their plans and procedures. They are sometimes rather hostile to the uninitiated outsider, however good his intentions, however deep his concern' (p. 107), and they add this generous concession to artistic temperament: 'Thus patience and acceptance of occasionally difficult personal relations is a necessity in supporting the arts' (p. 108).

Another method by which state support may be given is by tax concessions to firms and other bodies and individuals in order to achieve the same objectives – a subsidy to the provision of performance. There is, of course, much to argue about in discussing the relative merits of public as against private patronage in relation to artistic freedom. I confine myself here to two remarks. The first is that it is certainly true that tax concessions do not guarantee that any particular amount of funds will be made available in a given year. Whereas it could be argued that public support is equally uncertain in

amount and in rate of growth, at least public budgeting requires that
available amounts, however small, are known in advance. Tax law in
the US is particularly favourable to corporations supporting the arts
yet nothing like the full amount of the concessions available at federal
or local level is taken up. My second remark is that, provided these
concessions are not too restricted in their application, there is surely
a case for encouraging private endeavour and for diversifying the
number of sources of finance. This offers some hope to those who, if
unsuccessful in obtaining funds from one body, may fare better with
another. This possibility would be denied them in a society in which
private initiative was stifled and which offered funds only to those
who satisfy one patron – the state.

A final method for meeting the income gap is to use the power of
the purse to produce the shift in tastes and preferences necessary to
ensure that contemporary music will flourish because audiences of
sufficient discrimination and enthusiasm will be produced. Clearly
this can only be a long-term aim, because it postulates a change in
both the amount and form of musical education.

Perhaps a few words are in order here about the content of
such education, if this method were approved. A good deal of
contemporary music is like cricket – it arouses great enthusiasm and
tangible support from those who know how to play it. It may never
be possible to produce a large enough audience of young persons who
know the finer points of the game, but clearly audiences are likely
to be drawn from those who have a clear idea and appreciation of
its rules, and these will comprise mostly amateur musicians. I am
aware that there are now schools and other institutions which place
much more emphasis upon composition than hitherto and which
are attempting to destroy the hegemony of the diatonic scale which
so limits both performance and appreciation. One is on hazardous
ground in lecturing musicians on their own subject, but perhaps
the contemporary composers and musicians need to recognise that
public demand is essential for their survival. If they feel unwilling
to undertake the task of education themselves, they must not despise
the members of the Appreciation Racket, as Virgil Thomson has
christened them – critics and the like – who try to perform the task
for them.

Concluding Remarks

A very wise man has pointed to the dangers of what he has called
'esoteric isolationism in music', resulting in a secret language
understandable only to the initiated, and the alienation of the
ordinary music lover. Berating the profession he adds: 'never will
it occur to you that the composer may be guilty, that the consumers
are not the only ones to be blamed. You rather accept the situation
as an inalterable fact, grown out of historical necessity . . . . On this
basis you will not cease to make your complaints heard: the neglect

of our modern music is a burning disgrace; we shall not become the martyrs of the general conspiracy against our works! And then you meet with your fellow sufferers in international, national and local societies for contemporary music, you arrange festivals, symposia, and anything else for the propaganda of your products and those of your fellow highbrows . . . .' And at a later point he adds: 'the realistic part of the [musical] composition's life is very much dependent on external circumstances, and the creative musician must . . . possess a navigator's sense and knowledge in order to steer his craft through barriers, high seas and shoals – provided of course that it is seaworthy'. The writer is not a crabbed economist, but a noted composer – Paul Hindemith (1953).

It would be wrong to suggest that composers and musicians should compromise in standards in order to curry favour with the public, for example by devoting their time to producing 'pop' or film music. Nor do I believe that making it increasingly difficult for the musical public to understand the professionals must necessarily mean that they will all be reduced to penury.

However, if musicians want to see more public support for modern music or unfamiliar music, they must be prepared to do two things. The first is to recognise that it is poor strategy merely to complain about the ignorance of the rest of the world or to put much faith in the old trick of the music hall comedian who endears himself to his audience by insulting them. This offers little support to those of their friends who may be willing to take over the less glamorous tasks of lobbying local councils, helping to sell tickets and seeing that the standards of bookkeeping meet the requirements of public accountability, once government funds are available.

My second request rests on the hypothesis advanced earlier that modern music is for musicians, just as cricket is for cricketers. In the long run, therefore, the creation of a public is a function of ability and willingness to educate and in a fashion which fosters and encourages amateur performance, and not merely passive listening. Would it compromise composers too much to write not merely piano and recorder pieces but string quartets and chamber music which did not make immense technical demands? (Here I merely echo the thoughts of composers like Roger Sessions and Paul Hindemith.) Surely it would be a more worthy objective to ensure public support in the form of pump-priming operations rather than incur the suspicion that it was developing into a permanent charity. The 'income gap', therefore, may be reduced significantly in the long run if public tastes are bent in the proper direction by composers' own efforts in teaching and composition, as well as by the more immediate means of a well organised and articulate political lobby designed to influence both central and local government.

CODA

I was encouraged by the reception offered by the composers and impresarios at the conference who belied their reputation of being difficult people who would regard with contempt any observations on their craft by an interloper. On the contrary, I received useful constructive criticisms. Perhaps the main one should have been anticipated. Composers did not object to being regarded as like ordinary people who had a living to make and set store by improving their material prospects, but, like all professionals, they derived particular satisfaction from – in economists' jargon – maximising their reputation with their peer group.

The impresarios and the few public officials present were intrigued by 'Baumol's Law', that productivity gains were not possible to reap in musical production. It seemed to offer objective and technical evidence that public subsidies for orchestras and opera should be tied to the growth in their costs. Economists might be viewed from now on from a different angle, as a source of tangible support for their efforts, instead of being branded with the same reputation as the parsimonious British Treasury. More anon.

I had some difficulty in publishing the article, but eventually a fuller version than I have given here was accepted, to my delight, by my academic friend and colleague, Professor Richard Sayers of LSE, who edited *The Three Banks Review*. That review, now unfortunately defunct, took a broad view of economic questions and expected authors to write in respectable English intelligible to a wide professional audience. Besides, I was supplied with offprints which could be distributed to those unlikely to come across my ideas in the common or club rooms or at the dentist.

A copy fell into the hands of the Earl of Harewood, who was then heavily engaged in musical administration, and who had been asked to be on the lookout, so it turned out, for someone to undertake a difficult task for the Arts Council. Instead of a minor incursion into a rather unusual field in which to ply my trade, I was to find that I was about to embark on a long and extraordinary odyssey replete with incident. Peacocks are not supposed to fly for more than a few yards, but this one found himself making long flights into strange territory.

Before I take you on my first journey, I have to make amends for some misunderstandings about the economist's trade which were bound to arise in these early encounters. Fasten your seat belts.

3

INTERMEZZO (1)
Economics of Musical Composition in One Lesson

A SUSPECT PROFESSION

Ask a composer of music what (s)he does and (s)he will reply something along these lines: 'I write out instructions to musicians which are based on my view of what constitutes interesting sound patterns and often do so within the restrictions of certain rhythms laid down by dance forms such as the waltz or bolero. Here, let me show you something I'm working on. Here is the "plan" written on manuscript paper. It is actually a work for several instruments but I can give you some idea on my piano of how I would like it to sound. It's a fairly simple piece and perhaps, after one run through, you might like to try to hum the cello part.' The composer has an immense advantage. (S)he can build on our common experience for the large majority of us are familiar with musical sounds from an early age, many play or sing and can select and often predict what kind of music we enjoy. Like the lady who rode to Banbury Cross, nowadays we can all have music, a personal concert, wherever we go and whenever we like. Children are encouraged to write music for performance from a tender age. We can identify easily with what appears to be a glamorous profession, even with the early struggles leading hopefully to eventual public success and adulation. Our emotions are stirred also by glorious failure of composers now greatly appreciated but who die in obscurity or at an early age. I speak of myself as much as of others. I cannot listen to the Schubertian third movement of Arriaga's only symphony or to the Pastorale of his third quartet without thinking of the tragic loss to the world from his death at the age of nineteen. Of course, I am well aware that if you ask a performing musician about his/her hopes and ambitions and how far they have been realised – particularly at the end of a season of popular concerts – you will be told some home truths about what it is like to be perpetually on the road playing whatever you are told to play and fearful that lapses in intonation and phrasing may be noticed. The fact remains that you can fairly easily understand what a musician does and the contribution (s)he makes to your enjoyment.

Ask an economist what (s)he does and you are likely to have any explanation prefaced by an embarrassed cough and a shifting from one foot to another. 'How much time have you got?', (s)he asks, but you insist on a few sentences only. 'Well, I believe I'm a scientist observing human behaviour – yours and mine included – in the process of making a living – what people produce, what they earn from doing so, how they spend their money or save it and what the likely consequences are of their actions. I hope that I can detect uniformities in behaviour which make it possible for me to reach conclusions of general interest such as why some nations become richer than others, what causes booms and depressions and what our economic future might be like. Of course, unlike natural scientists I cannot conduct controlled experiments which have any chance of succeeding. There are strong moral objections to putting human beings in "cages" and even if they were to submit voluntarily to experiments it is more than likely that their behaviour would be quite different from normal if they know that they are being observed. I have to rely on statistics of their recorded earning, spending and so on and on questionnaires which, with rare exceptions like the Census, rely on freely given answers where there is no sanction if people don't tell the truth. Here on my VDU is a statistical table showing the rise in total earnings and a graph which shows the observed relation between the rise in earnings and the rise in saving.'

You would not be the first person to rush for the door wondering what had ever led you to enquire what economists did. Your reactions would be quite normal. Outrage at the idea that human beings might be observed like dumb creatures when we are all unique, sentient, sensitive beings. Scepticism at the scientific pretensions of the subject – the nineteenth-century American economist Francis Amasa Walker lamented the fact that 'few men are presumptious enough to dispute with the chemist . . . upon points connected with the studies and labours of his life; but almost any man who can read or write feels himself at liberty to form and maintain opinions of his own about trade or money'. Lack of concern at the fate of those who devote themselves to conjecture on economic questions, even if their cogitations may markedly influence our well-being. Whoever heard of anyone worried for the future of civilisation because a supposedly brilliant economist died young? I only know of one novel – Buchan's *Prince of the Captivity* – in which the economist receives star billing. The hero sacrifices his life in order to prevent the assassination of a world-renowned economist who has a brilliant plan for solving an international financial crisis. It is believed that Buchan was thinking of John Maynard Keynes – but then Keynes was a man of many parts who commands our interest through much more than his professional skills.

This is not to say that economists may not be interesting people and, as John Stuart Mill asserted, no-one is likely to be a good economist if (s)he is nothing more. But if musicians make good subjects for musical drama – Stradella (in Flotow's opera of that name) assassinated in Turin by the hirelings of a jealous husband, Orpheus in Gluck's opera seria and in Offenbach's satire, Salieri and Mozart in Rimsky-Korsakov's curious one-acter – I can only think of one economist in this category. The Scot, John Law of Lauriston, prolific writer on money questions and inventor of paper money, charming Parisian courtier and womaniser, started his colourful career involved in a romantic affair in which he killed his rival in a duel and joined the many interesting historical figures who died in Venice. The Professor of Economics at Harvard University, Richard Gill, who combined his teaching with being principal bass in the New York City Opera would have been an appropriate choice to sing the role, were he a tenor!

When faced with the double disadvantage of lack of literary talent and a subject which lacks glamour, the only thing to do is to press on and hope that I can at least convince the reader that my close encounters, brought into being through my professional activities, are of interest as an essay in persuasion.

ECONOMICS FUNDAMENTALS

A discipline claiming the status of a science must be based on some fundamental propositions. Fundamental economic propositions may seem tenuous and imprecise. There are two: (a) human beings' behaviour patterns are consistent and human nature is constant in time and place; and (b) every human choice involves a cost, represented by the alternatives forgone. It is a characteristic of brilliant scientific minds to question the fundamentals of their own subject or at least to consider the consequences of assuming that they may not hold. Characteristically, Keynes considered the prospect that, in the long run, the world would be so replete with resources that the problem of the alternative cost of one's actions would disappear; at the same time, the removal of this constraint on human action would transform human nature so that we would become more contented and more civilised human beings. But his argument was based on the strong assumptions that man would limit the growth in his numbers, wars would become less frequent, and people were prepared to listen to those, like himself, who could introduce them to the joys of the intellect and the imagination, which would include music.

There has been much misunderstanding of the first proposition, even by eminent philosophers. It is based on simple observations over the centuries, such as the familiar relation between the demand for some product and its price, but does not entail passing any judgment on the individuals' choices of goods and services or enquiry into the reasons why they buy them. No moral imperative requires an economist to judge the actions of individuals by specifying some 'hierarchy of choices' – that may be left to theologians and moral philosophers. There is a splendid little interchange between Benedetto Croce (the Italian philosopher) and Vilfredo Pareto (the Italian economist) in which Croce argues that economic actions can imply approval or disapproval but that one cannot do the same for a mechanical action, for example the movement of the foot. *Ergo*, according to Croce, economic facts cannot be examined in the same way as mechanical facts. Pareto replies that if one man kicks another, then the movement of the foot is a mechanical phenomenon, but the act itself may be subject to approval or disapproval; *ergo*, the distinction is otiose and observation by economists of acts of exchange are no different from observations by medical scientists. The use of economics to show how individuals rank their preferences for goods and services does not entail a statement about the value of their actions. When Oscar Wilde made his famous remark 'an economist is a man who knows the price of everything and the value of nothing', he was exploiting his talent to amuse, but was nearer the truth than he realised. 'An economist is a man who knows the price of many things but is not competent to evaluate pricing decisions' is a more accurate, but much duller statement!

I may have convinced you that an economist examining human actions sees himself in the modest role of an observer and calculator, but I know I shall have more difficulty in explaining the implications of the second proposition. It is known colloquially in the trade as the TANSTAFL principle – 'there ain't no such thing as a free lunch'. Every act of choice means weighing the benefits of the action against the benefits of some alternative course of action. Furthermore, there is no scientific way of deciding whether one course of action is 'better' than any other, and, moreover, one cannot even be certain that the course of action one takes has precisely the consequences that one expects. One can try to reduce the uncertainty attached to one's course of action by seeking more information about its consequences, but the acquisition of information itself involves costs in the form of time and money.

For example, in reading these sentences you have made a conscious subjective decision to keep awake. The information you have chosen to read would be bound to be imperfect, for it would be difficult for you to assess the anthropological characteristics of the author. You have chosen under conditions of uncertainty, and paid the cost in terms of the other things you might have done with your time and energy. The result may surprise and disappoint you, but at least you acquire knowledge of what sort of things economists think about, knowledge which may be put to future use!

My favourite example of the 'opportunity cost' problem is that of a talk given some years ago in a French colonial province by the French Minister for Development which some Berber tribesmen

were persuaded to attend. It was the Minister's custom to obtain
'feedback' from his talks about co-operation between villagers
and planners and an embarrassed official was asked to report
back to him what the tribesmen had thought about his speech.
Pressed for an answer, the official said: they thought that their
attendance had too high a cost because it had been a beautiful
moonlit night, so they had forgone perfect conditions for horse
stealing!

It is common for professions to have a code of conduct and in
medicine this goes so far as the taking of the Hippocratic Oath
on graduation. There is no counterpart amongst economists, but
I think that it is commonly accepted that we have the rather grave
responsibility of helping those we advise to consider and to face
up to the consequences of alternative courses of action which
require the use of physical resources and human skills.

Consider the following example of what Guido Calabresi, a
remarkable academic lawyer who employs economic analysis,
would call a 'tragic choice'. Under public pressure, a government
is obliged to seek ways of reducing fatal accidents on roads. If,
as we prefer to think, the value of human life is infinite, then
resources must be found and regulations introduced, which
would reduce the number of fatal accidents to zero. It is clear that
the resource cost of achieving this objective without preventing
people driving at all would be enormous. If any attempt is made
to prevent accidents by raising the cost of accident liability to
careless drivers as an alternative to investment in safer roads,
there would be an outcry at the restrictions which would be
necessary. In very poor countries, any attempt to reduce fatal
accidents on roads to zero would entail the use of scarce resources
which could result in people dying of starvation as an alternative
to being knocked down on the public highway. An analogous
situation arises in considering the implications of a health service policy which assumes that its object is to prolong human
life as much as possible. It is usually the poor economist who
has to think the unthinkable and take the responsibility of
giving voice to it – whether we like it or not we do price human lives. No wonder Thomas Love Peacock, the nineteenth-
century English novelist – no relation though I have adopted
him as an ancestor – called political economy 'a hyperbarbarous
technology'.

A less poignant example comes from my experience as Chairman of the Scottish Arts Council which offers a foretaste of some later observations (see p. 130). Imagine you have to preside over the division of a limited public budget for arts funding. One can perhaps accept that aesthetic judgments about the quality of artistic productions are best made by those who command the respect of their fellow professional artists, although, as an economist, one is bound to point out that even these informed judgments are matters of disagreement amongst those who claim to know what is 'good art'. However, a false step in the process of policy making is made if we defer to the judgment of such professionals on the allocation of resources to further their cherished projects. In the case of heritage projects we have a Royal Commission on Ancient Monuments in Britain which takes great pains to list buildings of historic interest and I suspect that they have enough work on hand to employ them for a century by which time the stock of 'heritage' will have been replenished by buildings now being constructed. The implications of this activity is that resources have to be found to preserve all the entries on the list. An analogous approach is implicit in those who make judgments on the output of new artefacts, musical compositions and plays, not to speak of the preservation of works already in existence. Our orchestras, our opera, ballet and theatre companies all complain about being 'underfunded' and sincerely believe that the term has some technical meaning. The optimal expenditure on cultural pursuits, as in our previous examples, is illimitable. A funding body, with limited resources, is forced to make unpopular, if not tragic choices, in which those who obtain funding claim they do not get enough and those who are refused funding claim that the funders neither know how valuable their contribution to society is nor care about their aspirations.

But the matter does not end there. Painters, musicians and writers are no exception to our first law of economics and employ their particular talents in trying to induce governments to exempt them from resource constraints; and these talents, as I have indicated are formidable. Only the sustained clamour by so many professions to be given special treatment by government makes it possible for politicians to resist the histrionic displays of outraged artists who call them 'philistines'. Worried at the growth in public spending and finance, in the late nineteenth-century, William Gladstone observed that 'the income tax is turning us into a nation of liars'. Bearing in mind the large number of supplicants for public funding from all sections of society, the corresponding aphorism today might be: 'the prospect of government subsidy is turning us into a nation of special pleaders'. Of course, the 'special pleaders' are always the others! 'I am underfunded, you are looking for a cash hand-out, he/she wants a pension for life', as the selective declension of 'to subsidise' might be stated.

You may be left wondering why any sensible person would want to be an economist. The training is hard, the scope of the subject is vast, the subject matter, human action, cannot be observed under controlled conditions, and so the practical results are in dispute. Worse still, more often than not, the conclusions reached are unpalatable, indicating that the imaginative schemes of industries and governments are often unrealistic. Do I hear the psychologists muttering, *sotto voce*, 'a clear case of sado-masochism?' One is almost forced to agree with them, for, the obvious alternative explanation – economists are paid more than others for being in a dangerous occupation – does not seem to be true. It is not even as if an economist's skills make them fortunes in business or on the stock market. 'As you are so smart, how come you are not rich?' is the common jibe of businessmen to economists. The reply is: 'being a ballistics expert does not turn one into a good tennis player'.

I think that there are two reasons why we survive and, indeed, may flourish as a profession. The first and most obvious one is that there is a demand for our services in all walks of life, even in the field of culture and the arts. We have our uses, even if we are regarded as a necessary evil. As the Nobel Laureate, Stigler (1991) has remarked, 'the tedious humour about the differences of opinion among economists . . . or our infatuation with abstract thinking are really envious jibes . . . . How much sweeter is envy than pity'. His words overemphasise, perhaps, our remoteness from those we try to advise and instruct. More often than not, economists are brought in as members of a team, searching for a solution to a common problem. Their contribution must not only be substantial but be seen to be such. While this may not always happen, when it does suspicion and envy give way to understanding and even admiration, however grudging.

The second is that there is no shortage of recruits either to the economics profession as such or to those professions where a knowledge of economics is perceived as useful. There seems to be an inherent attraction in studying a subject in which oneself and one's colleagues are part of the subject matter. The human instinct to analyse and to measure can be satisfied. If we derive satisfaction from trying to improve the welfare of others, economics appears to be of assistance, even if its role is to cast doubt on feats of human imagination. It is, after all, the economists who forecasted the inevitable breakdown in a brutal collectivism which has enslaved millions, though they failed to forecast when, where or how it would happen.

THE MARKET FOR MUSICAL COMPOSITION

Let me try to show you now how some of these fundamental ideas can be applied to the understanding of musical activity. Although I am concerned with the performance as well as the creation of musical works, it makes sense, I find, to build my analysis round the activities of the composer who is certainly a necessary though not a sufficient condition for musical performance. I am thinking primarily of 'serious' composers by which I have in mind writers of music who have undergone extensive training in composition with the object of producing 'major' symphonic or chamber works, musical drama or oratorio, and who seek to demonstrate that these works are 'original'. The word 'serious' implies a contrast with 'popular' composers who are primarily melodists writing slight pieces for the entertainment of a wide public. No 'ranking' of the activities of these distinct groups is implied. Indeed, such a ranking would have been difficult to make in the eighteenth-century and many well known 'serious' composers have gone out of their way to produce popular music as well. There are some signs that present-day post-modernist composers would question whether the distinction is necessary. In addition, some merging of interests has been fostered by mutual exploitation of new electronic devices (for details see, for example, Association of Professional Composers, 1989).

A musical composition is an essential component in a musical performance, and at one time was regarded as a prime example of a 'perishable' commodity. Thus Adam Smith (1776, Book 2, Chapter 3) characterised musical performance along with similar artistic productions as 'an activity which does not fix or realize itself in any permanent subject or vendible commodity which endures after the labour is past'. Whereas a live performance is a precondition for the realisation of a composer's attentions, it is now technically feasible to store music on disc and tape, and, in principle at least, the stock of musical composition can be maintained intact without the employment of a single additional musician after first recording. However, it is clearly an exaggeration to say that mechanical reproduction has completely killed off live performance, even if 'serious' musical performances are not characterised by the compelling gyrations on the stage of pop and rock stars. The sense of occasion still attracts audiences to the presentation of new works and new interpretations of old works – witness the vast interest in both the live performance and new recordings of eighteenth- and nineteenth-century works on original instruments.

The important point about the possibility of storing musical performance is that composers' interest in the presentation of their works must extend far beyond the confines of the concert hall or opera house. The pursuit of this interest is one of the more intriguing aspects of the market for musical composition.

A second characteristic of musical composition differentiates it from many goods and services in common use. Generally speaking, the use of most goods and services can be denied to those who are not prepared to pay for them, that is to say they have the qualities of divisibility and excludability. If I wish to drink a bottle of wine, I can normally be excluded from doing so if I am not prepared to pay for it. If I pay for it and drink it all myself, this denies other persons the possibility of enjoying it, although they may derive a vicarious satisfaction from seeing me relax and mellow in the process! The enjoyment (consumption) of music by an individual does not preclude another person enjoying its performance; the product is indivisible. At the same time, at least in the case of live performance, the enjoyment of music can be denied to those who are not prepared to pay. A market can therefore be established in performance. However, the position is quite different if we extend the definition of performance to include presentation through the medium of television, radio, home video cassette and disc. Once it is accepted that the composer has a right to some return from performance outside the concert hall, the 'principle of exclusion' becomes very difficult to apply. He may obtain some income from the commissioning of his work, its live performances and even the sale of the score, but deriving an income from other sources could involve the individual composer in incurring costs which far exceed the likely benefits in the form of increased income. This problem merits further investigation.

The first category of costs is of a fundamental character and applies to all publication and all performance of a musical composition. This is to establish legal protection for copyright in publication and performance of any kind. The history of the composers' struggle to establish these property rights is a subject in itself (for British experience, see Peacock and Weir, 1975; Ehrlich, 1989; and Chapter 6 below). It was only in the nineteenth-century, particularly as a result of the development of more rapid communication, that it was possible for a composer or his agent(s) to discover quickly whether or not his work had been performed – and then only in major musical centres – or whether 'pirated' editions had been published.

The example of the dissemination of Joseph Haydn's work in the eighteenth-century makes the point about establishing property rights very well. Circa 1760, Haydn's works were becoming known in England and France as well as in his native Austria-Hungary, but Haydn received no reward from the editions of his works published in those countries. Further, the French publishers passed off the works of other composers as those of Haydn. On the principle that 'if you can't beat them, join them', Haydn made direct contact with publishers in Paris, London and Berlin and offered new works to them direct. He then managed to sell rights to the same symphonies in these different musical centres! (See Robbins Landon, 1980, Chapter 10.)

The second category of costs consists of the cost of discovering whether or not public performance of a musical work has taken place in a country where copyright is protected. It is one thing to institute monitoring arrangements for live performance but quite another to cover 'canned' performance by radio, television, cassette player and juke box.

The final category of costs is associated with the negotiation of 'prices' for publication and performance of works together with devising of some suitable means for collecting fees, once these have been agreed.

It is almost superfluous to add that, however favourable the law of any country might be towards the establishment of property rights in publication and performance, the definition of these terms frequently requires composers or their agents to seek the help of the courts, entailing legal costs.

It is now obvious that the combined effect of the dissemination of his work by the newer media and the complications associated with negotiating rights bring the composer into contact with a rather complicated pattern of economic transactions. To understand how composers react to this situation, the market for musical composition must be described and analysed.

It is only possible here to outline the main features of this market. Perhaps the best way to understand it is to realise that the composer has in the course of the last two centuries gradually moved 'upstream' in the production process of musical performances of his own works. Broadly speaking, until the early nineteenth-century the composer was in close touch with his public and participated in the performance of his own work, being therefore an executant as well as a composer. Mozart not only gave the first performances of his own superb piano concertos but took an active part in canvassing for subscriptions to his own concerts (cf. Robbins Landon, 1989, Chapter 6). Public performance may still remain a cardinal element in bringing a new work to the public's attention, but the composer's direct exposure to the public has gradually diminished. However, the extreme difference from the position 200 years ago lies in the influence of technical change which makes it possible for consumers of new music to arrange their 'own performance' of the work through purchase of or even hire of recordings and the use of the video-cassette recorder (VCR) to time-shift television performances to suit their convenience. With the disappearance of the composer as a necessary condition for the execution of his/her work and these technical advances, (s)he need have little contact with the audience.

The consequences of these changes for the configuration of the market are illustrated in Figure 3.1. The figure traces the 'paths' through which composers reach their potential market. At one extreme, composers may still perform, like medieval trouba- dours, to a live audience when, for example, they give piano recitals of their own compositions. An intermediate position is one in which an orchestra commissions a composition for live performance which is made available in manuscript form or which could be simultaneously published by a musical pub- lisher. At the other extreme the composer has a piece recorded by an orchestra, and a televised version is simultaneously recorded which a viewer/listener then records on a VCR to play at his/her leisure. There are other variants, too. Next to my desk, as I write this, is a pile of piano music by some living composers which I can perform at home, the only intermediary between myself and the composer being the publisher and retailer of the works.

The figure also indicates the growing complexity of the po- tential sources of income for composers. The troubadours, like door-to-door salesmen, usually took their money on the im- mediate completion of the service. However, modern composers are faced with the well known 'agency problem' identified by economists, in that they have to employ others to act for them in presenting demands for payment – normally the publisher of the music together with the 'performing right' agency that collects royalties for both publisher and composer, usually with a long time-lag. What the figure does not tell us is that composers have generally perceived themselves as being at the mercy of the agents and to a major extent this is likely to be true unless they are able to take combined action of some sort. This is because of growing reliance on the market perceptions of the broadcasting and recording companies. In the UK, for instance, whereas royalties for public domestic performances of musical compositions in 1989 reached £34m., royalties from radio and television, at £42m., exceeded this figure by £8m. (Unfortunately we cannot break these totals down according to type of musical composition.)

The potential disadvantage which the individual composer en- countered in being faced with powerful buyers of his/her prod- uct is compounded by another factor analogous to that faced by writers of novels. Up till the time of, say, Mendelssohn, the com- petition that a composer faced in a 'performance package' would be, broadly speaking, provided by his/her contemporaries. The

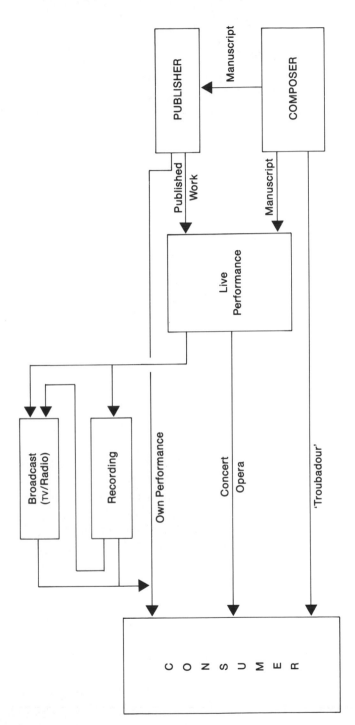

FIGURE 13.1:   The Market for Musical Composition.

present position is radically different and even a cursory examination of concert series by major orchestras and of programmes for an opera season would reveal that contemporary music forms a relatively small percentage of the repertoire (see Chapter 2). Moreover, prospects of anything more than a single performance of a new work are rare. 'The majority of new pieces, after having anemically overcome their premiere, hardly ever have enough stamina to stagger along to a second performance' (Paul Hindemith, 1953). It is claimed by some composers of my acquaintance that this lack of appeal of contemporary music may only be a transitory phenomenon, but the fact remains that a large proportion of royalties earned from musical composition accrue to the heirs of dead composers whose work remains in copyright for periods up to fifty years after their death.

THE COMPOSER AS 'ENTREPRENEUR'

The above description of the market for musical composition explains the actions of composers in trying to defend their economic position.

Individual Action

As we have observed in Chapter 2, the motivation of serious composers indicates that they do not derive utility simply by directing their efforts to producing music for the public's satisfaction. As with other professional groups, they derive utility from their reputation with fellow composers, normally achieved by their innovatory activities. (One has only to think of the immense influence of serial composition on mid-twentieth-century composers.) Accordingly, it comes as no surprise that composers have had to diversify their sources of income by moving further 'upstream' to exploit opportunities as teachers and 'downstream' as performing musicians, not primarily as performers of their own works. The empirical evidence of this is rather scanty. In the early 1970s I conducted the first known enquiry into composers' earnings for the UK Performing Right Society and some results shown in Table 3.1.

These figures clearly demonstrate that earnings from composition were heavily skewed. Taking median rather than average earnings, it was found that the total earnings of the median serious composer were almost exactly equal to the median

TABLE 3.1:   Earnings of 'Serious' Composers, 1971.

Sources of earnings		Earnings from musical composition as percentage of total earnings	
Source	*%*	*Ranges*	*%*
Musical composition	35.7	Less than 20 %	61.0
Other musical activities (e.g. teaching, performing, reviewing, conducting)	37.1	20 % to 80 %	25.0
Non-musical activities	27.2	Over 80 %	14.0

income of non-manual earners. In his report for the Arts Council of Great Britain, Alan Rump (1977) maintained that the position had not altered since 1971. I consulted the Association of British Composers about the contemporary position and, although they have no further data, their impression is that the position has not changed to any marked degree since I recorded my results. I am not in a position to report on comparable researches in other countries, but I would be surprised if the phenomenon of diversification of earnings by serious composers was not widespread.

It would be wrong to give the impression that the sole technique of composers, acting alone, is one of passive adjustment to market conditions. 'Cultural advertising' has been carried out by composers who have formed a close relationship with a particular opera group or orchestra as a means for performing their own works and those of close associates. It is certainly true that composers such as Britten, Menotti, Stockhausen and Henze have not used this technique solely in order to buttress their economic position and, indeed, it could be argued that it is only those who have been economically successful who have been able to take the risks; and certainly they have used their influence to benefit other composers. A novel variant of solidarity with the modern serious composer is instanced in Simon Rattle's announcement that he would not sign a contract with a well known record company unless it recorded the work of the British composer Nicholas Maw.

Co-operative Action.

Clearly, publishers of music and composers have a common
interest in monitoring performance of works, in order to exact
payment from beneficiaries. There are clearly large 'economies
of scale' derived from specialised 'production' of monitoring and
collecting royalties and the evidence for this is in the remarkable
growth in organisations engaged in these activities. Each major
country has at least one such organisation and there is close international co-operation in order to facilitate collection of royalties
for work in the international repertoire. Although it is not possible to identify the 'serious' composers and their publishers in the
statistics provided by the UK Performing Right Society (PRS), it
is staggering to realise that the PRS represent 750,000 copyright
owners of all nationalities alongside its own members who total
20,000 composers, authors (e.g. lyric writers and librettists) and
publishers of musical works. The acceleration in business by such
organisations was occasioned by the development of recording,
radio and later television companies which controlled the market
of 'canned' production of music before being challenged by the
growth of the countervailing power of performing right societies.
(For further analysis, see Peacock, 1979).

Collective Action

Bodies such as the PRS are concerned with negotiating prices
of performance and they are usually only incidentally concerned with influencing the size and composition of output,
although they have a strong interest in the legal definition of
what constitutes 'performance'. Collective action by composers
is more analogous with trade union or trade association activities
designed to influence both price and output. In the UK, the Composers' Guild has sought to influence broadcasters and concert
organisers to discriminate in favour of British works. Such a
body has also been very active in pressing for improvements in
government subsidies for music in general and for composers in
particular.

The last two forms of action invite the speculation as to whether
they inhibit freedom of entry into the market for musical composition. (I am ruling out the kind of situation which once
existed in Communist Russia by which composers could be

denied a livelihood by an order for expulsion by the Ministry of Culture!) Performing Right Societies commonly insist on two conditions before admitting a composer as a member. The first is evidence that they have had a quantum of work performed in public or commercially recorded or broadcast. The second is an entry fee – normally not very large. In the UK, the PRS divides members into two categories: (a) Associate Member and (b) Full Member. The distinction in membership rests on the amount of their earnings, and the difference in status entitles only Full Members to nominate and be nominated to the governing body (see Performing Right Society Ltd., 1990a).

On the whole, serious composers seem to be fairly satisfied with conditions for entry into Performing Right Societies, the main elements of controversy being associated with the system of disbursement of royalties, such as the division between publishers and composers and between the various categories of composers.

SOME CONCLUSIONS

The first question concerned the economic condition of composers. The romantic notion of a serious composer 'starving in the garret' or finishing up, like Mozart, with a pauper's grave is wholly misleading. (Incidentally, historical research has shown that both Mozart and Schubert, regarded as starving geniuses, earned respectively large and respectable sums of money towards the end of their short lives; see Robbins Landon (1988, Chapter XII) on Mozart and Reed (1972) on Schubert). Such evidence as is available on earnings, as we have seen, demonstrates that serious composers may be quite comfortably off. What is undeniable, however, is that if they were forced to rely on earnings from composition alone, then their economic condition would indeed be poor and precarious.

Our earlier survey points towards a further conclusion. It is doubtful if the quantity of musical composition is affected to any marked extent by economic conditions. It might be argued, however, that the diversion of composer activity to making a living by other musical activities or by non-musical activities militates against division of labour and could reduce the quality of output below that which would otherwise obtain if composers could concentrate on the activity in which they claim a comparative advantage. It might also be argued that the time profile of earnings forces the young and enterprising composers more likely to be willing and possibly able to exploit new ideas to reduce their 'investment' in experimentation. The argument can be pressed too far. There does not seem ever to have been a time when the majority of senior composers of any standing did not have to rely on earnings from sources other than composition or even on the incomes of others. It is not at all obvious that removal of obstacles to being able to spend more time on musical composition would result in an increase in quality. Would Charles Ives have been a better composer if he had not had to start out making a living as an insurance broker?

Let me return to the question I raised when I first considered public intervention to support composers (see Chapter 2). It is a common value judgment that public support for education and training should be a right, and that the student should be free to choose freely his or her subject of study. Furthermore, that right should extend to include at least the provision of a university or conservatoire training provided that the student has the ability and self-discipline to complete the course of study, or at least that a high probability of course completion can be expected. If that value judgment is accepted then those who wish to study, perform and write serious music should not be discriminated against.

However, the third conclusion I would draw maintains that the right to choose one's training for a profession does not extend to the guarantee of lifetime employment in the profession of one's choice. Other arguments have to be advanced for public support of some form for musical composition, support which would not otherwise normally be available to those in other professions. Such arguments are usually bundled together within the category of 'externalities' or 'uncovenanted benefits' which denote that musical composition has a value for society over and above the earnings derived from it by composers.

Whether such arguments are substantial and what they entail by way of public intervention beyond full or partial financial support for musical education is an important question, but I can only make my own views clear by returning to the odyssey which is the main subject of this book. That means taking the train from York to London.

4

MOLTO FURIOSO
Orchestrating Orchestras

BACKGROUND

At regular intervals, in practically every area of government expenditure designed to influence the size of a particular sector of the economy, impossible or at least difficult questions are asked about the size and composition of the components of the sector. Are there 'too few' or 'too many' motor vehicle producers, is the industry 'properly balanced', is the quality of output 'satisfactory', is enough attention being paid to training and so on? Governments seem to think that these are sensible questions to ask, being always under pressure to people the committees of enquiry seeking answers with those with a strong vested interest in the committees' findings. They commonly accede at least in part to such requests, not simply because governments are necessarily 'captured' by such vested interests, but because access to information which may help such an enquiry depends on the co-operation of those likely to be affected by the results. The problem of 'asymmetrical information' illustrates my earlier point about the difficulties of economic and social investigation. Even if the committee consisted of completely disinterested highly intelligent and knowledgeable people, close observation of the behaviour of those with an interest in their conclusions is likely to modify that behaviour. Information supplied by the industry or firm under investigation may be distorted, not by dishonest practice, though that can happen, but by its incompleteness. Information not asked for need not be volunteered. In principle, data or observations supplied by the affected parties could be cross-checked, but, in practice, the second fundamental law of economics comes into play – the opportunity cost of doing so. The subjective cost to the decision maker at the margin of one committee of enquiry has to be measured in terms of the best alternative use – possibly another, equally urgent, enquiry.

It is therefore not surprising that so many public enquiries, while they may contain new information and fresh ideas for others to ponder, come to rather vague conclusions about what might be done about the perceived problems. Further, even if the government has a genuine motive for investigation, and is not merely using a committee of enquiry as an excuse for inaction, it can always discount the committee's conclusions, if these are unpalatable, because the committee bears none of the costs of carrying them out.

A different perspective on the problem of the size and composition of an industry is offered by the economist who will ask the question: why not let the market decide? Provided that consumers are well informed about what they buy or can obtain information about choices without incurring large costs, and provided there is freedom of entry into the industry, thus allowing those with new ideas or ways of supplying goods more cheaply a chance of gaining custom, the size and composition of the industry is decided by those whom its products are ultimately designed to satisfy. Nor need the size or composition of the industry be fixed and immutable, for both will respond to changes in consumer preferences as tastes and incomes change. I shall argue the case for consumer sovereignty in more detail later, but here and now only wish to make it clear that I am well aware of its implications. 'Perfect markets' fulfilling the above provisos rarely exist. Firms prefer to be able to control the market, which is why producer interests argue strongly for 'orderly markets' in which potential rivals are excluded. Governments may have great difficulty in detecting and controlling monopolistic and restrictive practices. The costs to the consumer of reducing ignorance can be high – no producer advertising on TV has an incentive to inform one about rivals' alternative products. The 'contestability' of markets for new entrants varies enormously according to the risks of entry. Nevertheless, the alternative to seeking to attain the impossibility of perfection is to leave consumers at the mercy of inefficient producers or to sell their birthright to those, not only governments, who claim that they can make better choices for us than we can make for ourselves.

The same questions, the same modes of seeking an answer and the doubtfulness of the conclusions reached apply just as much in the arts as elsewhere, whether one likes it or not. As I write this, the Arts Council of Great Britain has just announced that it has 'set up a team to examine the location of orchestras and their national distribution, the artistic balance of their programming, the arrangements for broadcasting, and the most effective management structure for the BBC orchestras'. Nicholas Kenyon, controller of Radio 3, Jane Glover the conductor, Clare Mulholland of the Independent Television Commission and Kenneth Baird, Music Director of the ACGB, are worthy of our respect as, in various ways, concerned with the production of what musicians would recognize as high quality performances of 'serious' music, and their conclusions must not be pre-judged. I am bound to wonder how much further they will advance our thinking on the deployment of orchestral resources beyond that of the committee which I chaired some years ago covering similar ground. I shall try not to bore the reader with too much detail about this earlier enquiry but concentrate on the perennial difficulties which enquiries of this kind encounter, and how an economist tries to cope with them.

In early 1969 I was vaguely aware of the fact that professional musical organisations were pressing for an official enquiry into the future of symphony orchestras. Attention to their problems had been focused largely on the London scene and in 1965 Arnold (later Lord) Goodman became Chairman of a Committee on the London Orchestras on which interested parties were represented, including orchestral employers and employees, the Musicians' Union, the Greater London Council and the Arts Council of Great Britain. Their Report lead to the establishment of the London Orchestral Concerts Board through which finance from both the ACGB and the GLC was channelled and the activities of the London orchestras were regulated and monitored. One further result of these changes was an improvement in the working conditions of orchestral players in London.

It was not long before it became clear that what was happening in London would affect the whole country. For one thing, it drew the attention of musicians in regional orchestras to the even greater gap between their pay and conditions and those in London orchestras than had existed hitherto, and managements feared that their best players would be lured to the metropolis. For another, it raised the more general question of how the Arts Council, as a major funding body for music, should allocate scarce resources between the different regions and nations of Great Britain.

A further influence on the orchestral scene was the position of the BBC. In the late sixties, the BBC was the largest single employer of orchestral players and operated nine 'house' orchestras, exactly the same number as the regional and London orchestras supported by the Arts Council. It was estimated to employ one-third of all professional symphonic musicians. The BBC itself had been reviewing its policy towards orchestral music and in the forward-looking *Broadcasting in the Seventies* published in 1968 had itself raised the question as to whether it should continue to support nine orchestras of its own.

The following year, the regional interests pressed the ACGB to put in hand a national enquiry concerning the development of the country's orchestral resources and responded by drawing up, in consultation with the Regional Orchestras Advisory Committee, the terms of reference of such an enquiry. These were: 'to consider and make recommendations for the development and financing of the professional orchestral resources of Great Britain, with particular reference to 1. Public concert-giving, especially outside London. 2. Broadcasting, television and recording. 3. Opera and ballet requirements. 4. Training of young musicians. 5. The relationship of contemporary repertoire and the living composer to financial considerations.'

My becoming Chairman of the committee handed this hot potato was, I believe, entirely Lord Harewood's doing. He had read and apparently was taken by the effusion which is partly reproduced in Chapter 2. He recommended me to the Chairman of the ACGB, none other than the Chairman of the previous London Orchestras Report, Lord Goodman. Lord Goodman and John Cruft – Music Director of the ACGB – gave me the once-over at a very good lunch at the Savoy and were apparently satisfied. I was offered the chairmanship of the Orchestral Resources Enquiry (ORE) and accepted it with enthusiasm but with some apprehension. In retrospect the emolument – £500 – seems meagre even converted to today's prices, but I suspect that everyone concerned knew that I would have done the job for nothing. The experience and the interest were their own reward, and so it proved to be.

Faced with the list of committee members appointed by the ACGB, I was awestruck. There was the well known composer, Malcolm Arnold; Christopher Cory of the Welsh Arts Council; Myers Foggin, then head of the Royal College of Music; Sir William Hart and Alderman C. H. Lucas, both with immense experience and knowledge of the problems of regional orchestras; Colin Mackenzie, Chairman of the Scottish Arts Council and a great public figure in Scottish business and cultural life; John May, Secretary of the Orchestral Employers' Association, right at the hub of the orchestral world; Victor Olof, who had been Managing Director of EMI; Hardie Ratcliffe, General Secretary of the Musicians' Union and former orchestral player; Thomas Russell, once principal viola under Beecham and famous in his profession as the erstwhile orchestral manager of the London Philharmonic Orchestra; and Charles Tapp, businessman and music patron *par excellence*. Appointed as observers, in addition to John Cruft, were Roy Bohana, Christie Duncan and Kenneth Jamieson, music officials of the Welsh, Scottish and Northern Ireland Arts Councils respectively; Ian Thom from the Department of Education and Science; and last but by no means least, Eric Thompson, Deputy Music Director of the ACGB, who was effectively executive director of our whole operation. The team was completed by Rosemary Dixson as Secretary and John Lazarus, a York graduate student, as Research Assistant – a post invented by me.

I consoled myself with several thoughts. The first was that, from our very first meeting, there was an immense amount of goodwill and recognition of the fact that the task we were faced with did entail examination of economic issues with which I could claim to be familiar. The second was the coincidence of having to chair this committee during that rare event, a sabbatical year, during which, in any case, I had an interest in looking further into the economics of cultural policy. I had more time to think than would otherwise have been possible. The third was a conviction that, as I have tried to indicate, economics is a 'technique of thinking' as Keynes called it, which at least enables one to construct a framework of analysis, although whether the framework would be recognisable as the one we should adopt was another matter.

The strenuous but enjoyable times that we had as a committee would tempt anyone to be anecdotal, but it is the results of our efforts rather than how we struggled to produce them that is relevant to my general theme. If I merely acknowledge my profound debt to them, and say very little more about their individual contributions, it is not because of any lack of appreciation.

GETTING ACQUAINTED

What follows has been written with the benefit of hindsight, so that the reader can be spared a plaint about the personal problems one may face as chairman of a committee of highly articulate, knowledgeable and sometimes opinionated (in the best sense) persons. It is the chairman's job to try to create order out of the plethora of ideas and opinions emanating not only from committee members but also from the host of those who have been asked or have sought to give evidence. In my experience it is fatal for a chairman to sit back and listen, though listen (s)he must to all and sundry, and then to try to arrive at some 'sense of the meeting' which so often results in a muddy and therefore suspect compromise. The chairman must work out, as far as possible in advance, the logical framework of the enquiry's Report, though without pre-judging its conclusions and how they are to be arrived at. Any enquiry is subject to major resource constraints such as the budget available for meetings and empirical investigation and the price of members' time. A framework is essential in order to maximise the use of limited resources. But one is maximising under conditions of uncertainty concerning such matters as who will be able to attend meetings, the unanticipated snags which may produce delays in data collection and presentation of evidence, and the extent to which members are agreed on the agenda encased in the framework, once this becomes apparent. The framework has to be both acceptable and flexible. In short, the chairman must be in the lead, and seen to be such, anticipating where there are likely to be difficulties and responsive to advice on how to overcome these, all of which must be manifested in quick and early drafts of the main ideas of the Report, so that members' minds can be wonderfully concentrated in a way which fully utilises their expertise and experience. All this calls for personal qualities, such as good humour, tolerance of criticism and patience, which, added to the requisite intellectual capacity and imagination, makes the paragonic chairperson a rare being. (I am particularly known for a short fuse – a great disadvantage!)

A committee has first of all to agree on the objectives, if these are not spelt out by those who invite them to give advice. Often this entails that the chair has to seek to articulate the value judgments of the individual members on policy questions. It comes as no surprise at all to find that the members of the ORE all believed that the devotion of more resources to orchestral activity and wider distribution of these resources to improve access to orchestral music were 'good things'. Our reasons, of course, might differ and it was understandable if the musicians amongst us had preferences influenced as much by the perceived need to keep musicians in employment and to improve their material prospects as by the perceived benefits accruing to listeners to music. Nor do I think that we were worried much by the fact that our views were based on subjective judgments.

For several members of the committee, it seemed entirely reasonable that 'what was good for musicians was good for the community' – a variant of the old argument 'what's good for General Motors is good for the US'. We could then get down to the business of reviewing the orchestral scene, revealing its 'deficiencies' and devising suitable arrangements to improve matters. There are many precedents in Arts Council pronouncements which follow this procedure (see King and Blaug, 1973). I was not content with this, and tried to persuade the committee, only with partial success, that, unless we believed that we were the arbiters of cultural tastes and claimed to know better than others what they should prefer, then we were bound to offer reasons why we believed that it was in the public interest not only to provide grants to orchestras in order for them to operate at a level of activity which might not otherwise result from the public paying through the box office, but also why such grants should be increased. To my mind, this meant reviewing the arguments put forward for orchestral subsidies, many of which I found naive and illogical.

Here are the relevant excerpts from the memorandum which I circulated to the committee:

1.   The existence of a subsidy to orchestras implies that money is being diverted from private pockets to public use, and that this money would be spent in an entirely different way than would be the case if the subsidy did not exist.

2.   How can subsidies be justified?

I   Pragmatic arguments

(i)   *Government 'waste'*: Government spending is a large proportion of total spending and, given no change in taxes, it would still be possible to divert money to music without reducing the 'output' of existing services. This is because the government is a 'wasteful' spender, e.g. Concorde, defence contracting.

This argument can be supported only if two assumptions hold: that in fact it can be proved that 'output' elsewhere would not be reduced (very difficult to do empirically), and that it is accepted that if diversion of funds to music can be performed without reducing output elsewhere, the community benefits *more* from extra spending on music compared with other competing forms of spending, e.g. health services.

(ii)   *Extra spending 'worth it'*: Even if taxes would have to be raised in order to increase expenditure on orchestras, it would be 'well worth the money'. This is argument by persuasion, but there is no reason why all members of the community would agree that the private consumption (or other public consumption) forgone should be given a lower valuation than the extra support given to music. Presumably if there were consensus on this matter, extra money would be forthcoming anyway.

(iii)   *'Taxation according to benefit'*: Governments, and particularly local governments, already provide services for special groups, e.g. sports facilities for sportsmen, libraries for readers, etc. Why not for music lovers? Even if music lovers are relatively well-off, why should they not benefit from the relatively higher share of the tax burden which they presumably bear? If this argument is accepted, then presumably it would involve a shift in government expenditure from other services to music so that, with no changes made in the structure of taxation, the 'poor' would lose out to the 'rich'. So the argument becomes one about the distribution of income – one has to make some evaluation of the greater inequality of income produced by the alteration in the expenditure 'mix'. There is no *technical* way of making this evaluation. One possible gloss in this argument is that presumably a subsidy could be devised which would both offer more support for music *and* not alter the income distribution, e.g. by providing subsidies which benefit the relatively ill-off. This would require a shift in subsidies from the producer to the consumer. It must be noted, however, that if the income distribution is not to be altered, the 'poor' have some services cut and are compensated by the expansion of music services. But is this what they want? How does one evaluate the 'loss' to, say, sports enthusiasts against the 'gain' to music-lovers?

(iv) *'The importance of being unimportant'*: Money spent on the arts is negligible anyway, and spread over the whole community, extra finance to provide better musical services would not be 'noticed'. There is an immediate practical objection to this argument, which is that relative size of public expenditure is not the criterion which determines whether or not the Public Accounts Committee or Select Committee on Estimates scrutinises central government expenditure, and already the Estimates Committee have had a searching look at the arts (see *Eighth Report of the Estimates Committee, Parliamentary Session*, 1967/68). But even if the expenditure were not 'noticed', there is still the problem that central government expenditure is given to the arts as a whole, and the claims of extra finance for music must be weighed against the claims of other arts. The evaluation of the competing claims again is a matter of judgment.

(v) *'Foreign governments spend relatively much more than we do'*: This is again argument by persuasion – shaming the 'uncultured' British into spending on the arts! The reason why foreign governments are able to spend relatively more is because they spend relatively less on other things, for, broadly speaking, public spending is just as large a proportion of total spending in Britain as in other major countries. There is no technical reason why government spending patterns should be the same in all countries. There are well known cases where the pricing system does not adequately reflect benefits to the community, quite apart from its effects on the other objectives of policy which we have listed. The main reason has nothing to do with the argument that people do not know what is good for them (cf. II below), but that certain goods in general demand cannot be provided through the market, or at least not very easily. These goods are characterised by 'indivisibility', that is to say they cannot be made available in divisible amounts to individuals, but can only be supplied as an indivisible whole available equally (more or less) to all. The common textbook example is the lighthouse. When it throws out a beam, every ship within reasonable distance can see it. However, to provide the service, it would be impossible to 'price' lighthouse services, for it is impossible to deny the benefits to those who are not prepared to pay. Put it another way, given no-one is compelled to pay, there is no guarantee that voluntary contributions would sum up to the amount required to provide the service, for no-one is obliged to reveal what he is prepared to pay rather than do without the service. Consequently, lighthouses are (or were) financed by compulsory levies and normally provided by governments.

The question for us is whether the same kind of indivisible element characterises orchestral services, resulting in their 'under-provision' if left to the market. (A related and more difficult question not dealt with here, concerns how much these services are under-provided, if it can be established that they are.) Clearly, orchestral services can be denied to those not willing to pay for them, so what has to be established is that the community obtains some benefit over and above that enjoyed by those who go to concerts, and a benefit which is exclusive to orchestral music.

Some of the pragmatic arguments are designed, I suppose, to persuade us that there are such benefits, but as already observed, they run into a number of objections. One can imagine that those not prepared to pay for enjoyment of the arts in general and music in particular do get some sort of benefit from the international prestige of the Royal Ballet, and from the indefinable improvement in the 'quality of environment' resulting from a cluster of cultural activities carried on in fine buildings. Also, if we consider that community benefit should be defined to cover the benefit of future generations, as well as the present one, there seems to be a case for subsidies.

As Baumol and Bowen have argued, 'few of us are willing to take the responsibility of passing on to future generations a country whose beauty has been destroyed' (1966, p. 384). This 'conservation of cultural resources' argument assumes that the arts, once destroyed, cannot be re-created, which is questionable, although one could maintain that the costs of re-creation may be high. But the trouble with all these arguments is that if they *are* so persuasive, why are the public not willing to pay more in taxes for the arts?

II 'Sociological' Arguments
I cannot claim to have anything more than a superficial acquaintance with sociological thinking, but I am fairly certain that this is the way some British sociologists would argue. There are certain 'needs' which have to be satisfied if society is to remain a stable entity, and to which everyone is 'entitled'. Among these are cultural needs. The 'recognition' of these needs is not guaranteed to all members of society, so that if people are poor, they are likely to remain so, because they are ignorant of the means by which they can be relieved of poverty. Even if they are subsidised, e.g. by social security payments, they are likely to make the 'wrong' choices because of their social and cultural background. Consequently, the problem of poverty cannot be solved purely by altering the income distribution and leaving people to look after themselves, but requires that the government choose for them and, as in the case of education and some forms of public health, people must be 'forced' to consume certain products. The same is true of 'cultural

poverty'. Consumer ignorance is sufficient argument for large-scale government intervention not merely to offer people the means to buy cultural 'goods' but also to *provide* the services themselves and at a subsidised or at a zero price. Cultural paternalism is a necessary means to an important end – the 'good' society. The policy solution is then to have the cultural expert to decide on the means and then to tax the community accordingly. There are at least three problems associated with this line of reasoning. The first is that what constitutes a 'good' or 'stable' society is not easy to specify. Nor is it technically easy to establish that, once defined, some sort of cultural ration will achieve the end in view. Lastly, it is an open question how far, given our existing political institution, the community at large will *allow* others to choose for them without let or hindrance, and for an indefinite period. In the extreme case of government by expert, the fanatical believer in the sociological argument, as I have put it, would deny the need for democratic government.

There is one strand in the sociological argument which can readily be joined with the 'economic' argument. Even those who support consumer choice as the safest guide to public taste accept that taste is a matter of education and that minors should be exposed to the benefits of culture so that, if they reject or accept them, at least they do so with knowledge of their qualities. It seems reasonable to assume that young people at the taste-forming stage are not suffering from over-exposure to music!

III   How should we argue our case?

We could, I suppose, simply ignore the question, why subsidise orchestras, and consider how far we could agree on the future pattern of orchestral activity and its implications for finance. I believe that this would be to avoid the issue, because I do not see how we can arrive at any rational conclusion about orchestral development without returning to first principles.

My first thoughts on the problem lead me to an argument something like the following. We should recognise that we are a pressure group who share the 'value judgment' that orchestral music confers important benefits on the community as part of the complex pattern of culture, although we probably differ among ourselves as to the extent to which these benefits accrue to the community at large other than concert-goers. As a minimum, therefore, we may be able to agree that the public at large, and particularly younger persons, are hardly in a position to make up their minds on the cultural benefits of orchestral music, given the very unequal distribution of orchestral resources, and that at least there is a short-run case for subsidies, if only as a means of 'bending' taste. This argument alone suggests important changes in both the amount and form of subsidisation, which need to be discussed at some length.

The longer-run case is more difficult to argue, especially as none of us would presumably forecast that the process of 'bending taste' will be so successful that subsidies will eventually become unnecessary. The ultimate positive test of the value of the community benefit is whether or not taxpayers and ratepayers will be willing to pay an ever-increasing amount for the arts, and music in particular. I do not believe that this proposition has been adequately tested, but I hazard the opinion that their willingness to do so may be very much influenced by *who* is going to benefit directly and *where*.

Nothing in what has been said solves such an important problem as the relative size of the contributions of central government, local government and the box-office. Nor am I assuming that there would be no changes in the size, structure and functions of the orchestra in the future. These matters clearly need our attention, but I believe we should clear our minds on the purpose of subsidies first.

The subsequent discussion of my memorandum was sympathetic and the logic was not disputed. However, the realities of the orchestral scene were that orchestras, along with a whole host of performing arts organisations and creative artists, were receiving public subsidies – as much as 50 per cent of their income from local and central government sources in the case of regional orchestras – and that it was not unreasonable to suppose that, in an admittedly centralist democracy, a public consensus had been registered that these subsidies were desirable. Even if we all agreed that the case for subsidies was 'not proven', we would lose credibility if we did not start with the existing situation rather than with some hypothetical one in which subsidies were assumed not to exist. The musical world and the public at large would at least be in a better position to make up their own minds if we stated our value judgments explicitly, examined in some detail the proposals which we believed consistent with such judgments and tried to estimate their costs. In any case, a strongly held belief that the expansion of orchestral services was a good thing did not preclude consideration of how that might be done by stimulating 'consumer demand' rather than by relying solely on direct public subsidy to orchestras.

The pragmatic position taken by the committee did not resolve my own personal dilemma, given my doubts about the general case for subsidies based on some uncovenanted benefit to society which is not reflected in what its members were willing to pay voluntarily for enjoyment of music. I went along with it because the credibility of my position with musicians depended on their conviction that, so far as music was concerned, I knew what I was talking about. I had before me a unique opportunity to show the relevance of economic analysis to the musical scene, whatever the initial judgments made about the desirability or otherwise of public support. Besides, I had already relaxed one important assumption in the traditional economic analysis which throws doubts on the justification of public support for the arts based on the sovereignty of the customer, namely that consumer tastes and preferences are a datum uninfluenced by the process of consumption (see Peacock, 1969). Economic analysis, up to this point, had had little to say about the *formation* of tastes and preferences and its implications for consumer welfare. There could be a case for public support of some kind for the formation of cultural taste which could satisfy a liberal conscience.

I received some good-natured ribbing from my fellow liberal economists who were and still are sceptical about any form of government funding of cultural activities with Tibor Scitovsky (1972), a well known welfare economist and strong supporter of the arts, claiming that I was a 'striking illustration' of 'the conflict between the music lover and the good economist'. I liked the bit about 'the good economist', but, as I indicate later, I have never been completely satisfied with his persuasive attempts to develop the argument about taste formation far beyond that to which I had made reference both in my 'subsidy memo' and in professional publication.

DIAGNOSIS

Whatever lingering doubts I may have had about the words in my Foreword to our Report (ACGB, 1970) that 'we all share the value judgment that it would be a body blow to cultural development in this country if . . . government would ignore the case for continuous and growing support for symphony orchestras', I set to work with a will to offer what I suppose is the first professional analysis of the economic environment of the orchestra for Britain. It formed the core of our diagnosis of the problems facing musical production and grew directly out of the argument advanced in Chapter 2, so it amounted to a discussion of the relevance of 'Baumol's Law' to British conditions.

Let me begin with the demand for orchestral music. It came

as a surprise to orchestral managers and players that, despite the growth in the relative proportion of funding received from central and local government sources, the proportion of works of living composers in orchestral programmes had, if anything, slightly declined between the 1930s and the late 1960s – the dead refused to lie down! The remarkable growth in orchestral audiences had made virtually no difference to the composition of the demanded repertoire. Furthermore, our best guess, based on a plethora of evidence from orchestral managers in London, the Regions, Wales and Scotland, was that the foreseeable future would see only a marginal increase in that proportion (see ACGB, 1970, Chapter 3). Large-scale nineteenth-century and early-twentieth-century works would continue to dominate programmes. (Before me is the Royal Scottish Orchestra's 1992–1993 Winter Season Programme for the Usher Hall in Edinburgh. There are seventy works, only five of which are by three living composers – Dalby (1), Hamilton (1) and Lutosławski (3)!)

The composition of the repertoire is the factor which brings into being the 'Iron Law of Baumol', for 'labour-saving innovations' cannot be introduced, the composer having specified down (up) to the last horn-player the labour input. Factor substitution – recording the horn parts in advance and 'mixing' them in with the live performance – would destroy the product. If the major cost factor in the production of orchestral music is the orchestra itself, and this cannot be disputed, then costs will be a positive function of musicians' wage rates per orchestral session. Orchestral activity could only expand if orchestral income rose *pari passu* and the wage bill would have to rise at a relatively greater rate than the wage bill in sectors in which productivity gains matched wage increases, unless the wage rates of orchestral players fell relatively to those in these other sectors.

You can well imagine how popular Baumol became with arts administrators struggling to find cogent arguments for increasing government funding (and therefore increasing their prestige and power) for the performing arts in general, though Will Baumol himself has denied that it was ever his intention to use his analysis to support any particular policies (see Baumol and Baumol, 1984). While there is no doubt that the ORE were impressed by the argument, its application to the British orchestral scene only dealt with part of our concerns and itself depended on assumptions about the activities of both performing and creative musicians which certainly had to be tested.

The first assumption requiring examination concerned the fixity of the repertoire. Those representing and supporting chamber orchestras could point out that their repertoire of both (largely baroque) older and new music required smaller forces and, in the case of the former, the 'factor input' could be very flexible in terms of both size and instrumentation. The ORE were very sympathetic to chamber orchestras, particularly as they had the additional advantage of being able to play in isolated places in venues not suitable for a symphony orchestra. However, even if we probably regarded them erroneously as 'niche bands' supplementing rather than replacing symphony orchestras, the fact was and still remains that, looking over the whole musical scene, the large orchestra, both performing on its own and for opera productions, is still the major player.

If the chamber orchestras brought a significant if not major change in the repertoire, particularly of baroque music, possibly a more interesting question we had to face was whether or not replacement of the 'standard repertoire' might take place because we underestimated changes in taste. The commercial theatre has survived because the public look for a large proportion of new plays rather than 'classics', but, significantly, there is clear evidence that the cast size of new plays has diminished, ignoring, of course, large musicals relying on star performers with drawing power. Could not a similar trend operate in music, with modern works being produced with smaller resources, but without a reduction in the public's perception of the quality of orchestral output?

We had to listen to a *'dialogue des sourds'*. Orchestral managers were quite damning about the attitudes of modern composers. To paraphrase a general view, modern composers wrote extremely difficult works usually requiring vast orchestral resources and a much larger input of rehearsal time. Worse still, composers were unconcerned by the fact that their works would normally have no audience appeal. They seemed to regard the orchestra as a medium for laboratory experiments in sound, with the audience – remembering Schoenberg's quip (see p. 25) – other than a few cognoscenti, only present on sufferance. Modern works if substituted for standard repertoire simply raised their costs and reduced orchestral income. At most, playing modern works might perform a useful function as shock therapy, which would act as a leaven to the staple diet and perhaps improve the production of that diet.

Composers were equally damning about orchestral managers, though, as we shall see, they are far from being the only targets of their tongue and pen. Malcolm Arnold singled out conductors, consumed by their vanity and the cash nexus, for particular blame. I recall him saying that modern orchestras would appoint a well-trained one-armed gorilla as a conductor if he brought in sufficient opportunities for recording and film work. However, a much more profound question was raised by composers and by the conductor Pierre Boulez. This was that the orchestra, like the opera, was becoming a 'museum piece'. The composers as innovators in sound patterns and in their search for new media for displaying these patterns were less dependent, at least technically, on the symphony orchestra. There was a distinct element of wish-fulfilment in this argument. This was not a case where supply would determine the demand for musical composition unless composers made more concessions to popular taste. However much one would want this to happen, the committee did not predict that it would, and subsequent events proved it right. Composers, however, as I have argued above, are much concerned about their reputation with their peer group and if they refuse to produce works which earn them a living, then they have to either rely on financing themselves from other activities, or lobby for public funding to be distributed according to peer group advice. Included in public funding sources is the BBC, of which more anon.

Of course, these discords could not be resolved. The debate is as old as orchestral music. But the basic issue was clear to us. The orchestra would remain the main mode of introduction of new works, either in live performance or in recordings and broadcasting, and would require inducements to present such works. At the same time, something would have to be done to 'move the composer downstream' to be in contact with his/her potential audiences, and to encourage potential and actual audiences to acquire the knowledge which would make them more appreciative of the efforts of musical innovators.

These thoughts are commonplace nowadays but were rarely voiced a quarter of a century ago.

If supply would not create its own demand, one had still to consider how far adjustments in demand might compensate for the rise in orchestral costs. This was not such an easy matter for investigation as might be thought. Firstly, one must recall that at the time quantitative economic research on long-run consumer trends was limited, and detailed investigation and projection of leisure consumption practically non-existent. Once we made our own calculations of the probable rise in orchestral costs resulting from our policy recommendations it soon became clear that the growth in box-office income necessary to finance our recommendations was well out of the range of possibilities. This result would be reinforced by our prior objective of greater equality of access to orchestral music within the regions and nations of the UK which would both raise costs and also lower potential box-office below what it might otherwise be if orchestras were free to maximise audiences. Secondly, as Figure 3.1 demonstrates, access to orchestral performance is also obtained through broadcasting. The BBC financed by a compulsory licence fee could offer orchestral supply without reference to box-office, but, in principle, there was no reason why it needed to be both an orchestral employer and transmitter of music. There appeared to be no clear principle governing the BBC's use of its own orchestras to provide broadcasts (generally of live performance) and other British orchestras. There was certainly no indication that the BBC regarded itself as being the guarantor of a given slice of future income for outside orchestras, including chamber orchestras, and its own live concerts, with highly subsidised ticket prices, produced 'unfair' competition.

If we had followed precedent, we could have used the excuse of ignorance to avoid making any calculation of how much our recommendations would cost, but I was determined that we should make a stab at costings. These were bound to be questioned, misunderstood and misused, as indeed they were, but an enquiry financed by public money and recommending further public expenditure can only offer the makings of a sensible debate on its deliberations if at least it examines the budgetary implications. The results of the costings can be summed up by saying that 'The Iron Law of Baumol' was clearly in evidence

and any countervailing forces would make little difference to the
income deficit for orchestras.

RECOMMENDATIONS

Our terms of reference required us to make a draft of recommendations and there were twenty-six in all. Looking at
Figure 3.1, they could be classified according to the stages of
musical production. Several were designed to bring the composer nearer to his/her audience, e.g. by composer-in-residence
schemes with both orchestras and educational institutions, and
to sustain young composers by grants and fellowships. Several
were designed to improve the flow of information between the
'live' and 'canned' sectors of orchestral production so that the
potent influence of the BBC could at least be anticipated in
orchestral planning. Several very sweeping recommendations
covered the efficiency and morale of orchestras, particularly
those proposing what nowadays are called 'mission statements'
backed by 'corporate plans' in which players would have a say.
Important, too, under this heading was the chance to give players
the opportunity to be members of smaller 'sinfoniettas' which
presented their talents more directly to audiences and also made
for more flexibility in reaching audiences in smaller centres.

A fourth set of recommendations were particularly in harmony
with my own view of methods of subsidy and I was particularly
pleased that these appealed to us all. They reflected the view
that the ultimate beneficiary from music, and also the ultimate
payer calling the tune, should have a distinct say in what should
be played and who should play it. Therefore, a greater proportion
of public funding should be channelled through the consumer
by awards to music societies made by regional arts associations
who could thus enable them to engage orchestras and agree with
them the programmes. A related recommendation was tax relief
for companies and individuals who wished to sponsor orchestral
concerts.

However, the two principal recommendations and the ones
which excited considerable controversy owe their origin to the
professionals on the ORE who were deeply concerned about the
quality of orchestral playing and the international reputation
of British music. It reflects a debate amongst economists which
goes far back in time, and which has not been resolved, namely

whether the incentive to offer efficient service is best achieved by the spur of competition or by stability in employee contracts, or by some combination of both. What was not disputed was that differential pay and conditions between orchestras would be reflected in complementary differences in the standard of playing.

Accordingly, the first of these recommendations was that public support should reflect the desire to make playing in regional orchestras as attractive as possible in comparison with London orchestras, which should be done by raising earnings in regional orchestras to the same level as for comparable work in London. The second recommendation was designed to be complementary to the first. Direct subsidies should be given to only two of the four London orchestras and geared to the requirement of accepting contractual arrangements for players which would ensure permanence and stability. This would not preclude the remaining two orchestras from being eligible for grants for public concerts and might encourage them to travel in response to the finance that we recommended should be made available to music societies and orchestral associations in parts of the UK other than London. The recommendation was clearly influenced by the contractual arrangements which applied in major symphony orchestras abroad who had reduced the opportunity cost of moonlighting and freelance work by providing good pay and conditions and ample time for private practice and rehearsal. A move in this direction would bring into question the suitability of player-managed orchestras with hiring and firing of administrative staff in the hands of a board of directors elected by the players.

I have only briefly outlined the main recommendations. There were many more touching the education of orchestral players, the role of local authorities in support of music, the orchestral needs of ballet and opera, and so on. These, too, will have a familiar ring to them, for they, like our main recommendations, are still the subject of speculation and controversy even after a quarter of a century.

AFTERMATH

While I believe that I can reasonably claim that our report became a landmark in the discussion of public policy towards music, the first explicitly to translate policy objectives into the resources required to fulfil them and to forge a clear link between policy aims and the appropriate financial instruments, its immediate 'fame', if that is the right word, lies in another direction. It is noteworthy in the history of cultural policy in the UK for having had its main recommendations rejected in advance of publication by the Council, and, moreover, despite the support given us by its own Music Panel. Lord Goodman, as Chairman, offered us the choice of revising our recommendations or of having them publicly rejected if we chose to leave them as they were. The committee were incensed at what they regarded as blackmail. The Council could hardly have had time to study the Report and, even if they had, surely any pronouncement on its contents should be made after consideration of professional and public reactions. (The Report was submitted in mid-April 1970 and I learnt of the Council's reaction at the end of May.) To a man we agreed that we would stand by what we had written, save for a few minor revisions suggested by the Music Director.

Worse was to follow. I specifically asked for any disclaimer by the Council to be issued separate from the Report. I wrote to John Cruft that 'I do not think that the Committee would like to be branded as well as disowned'. There was no reply to this request and the disclaimer appears in a 'Preface'(!) written by Lord Goodman. There are some honeyed words in this 'Preface', sincere and well-meant no doubt, but the message is unmistakable. Making orchestral playing more attractive outside London by using the pricing system was rejected because it 'seems not to be in accordance with governmental and commercial practice in some fields other than the arts'. Our proposal for a radical alteration in orchestral finance in London was damned by what is known as 'Cornford's Principle of Unripe Time'. This was a recommendation which, to quote, 'having regard to the current musical situation, the Council had not felt able to endorse at this moment in musical history'. Lord Goodman also rejected the proposal for tax relief to individuals and firms as a suitable way for marrying public support with private preferences, again on the grounds of not being in accordance with government and commercial practice. We can all change our minds. He certainly did and today is one of the most prominent supporters of business sponsorship for the arts buttressed by tax concessions!

It would be to adopt too conspiratorial an attitude to the Arts Council to suggest that the disclamatory preface was designed to divert press attention away from the rather fundamental issues raised by the report about arts funding; but it certainly had that effect. Examining contemporary press reports after many years, I am struck by the extent to which musical pundits of the time, noted for their metropolitan provincialism, took their cue from the rejection of the proposals for the London orchestras. The regional question, to them, was unimportant. I do not recall one well informed criticism of our analysis of the economics of orchestras, and some pundits clearly resented and possibly feared entry into the contemporary debate on musical matters by those trained to collect and to interpret empirical evidence, even if we were aware of the sensitivities of the subject matter. (Recall Chapter 2 on this point!). An article in the *Guardian* came nearest to scrutiny of our economic arguments, but was full of errors of fact and analysis and even claimed that we had 'blithely ignored' the cost of our proposals, whereas a whole chapter of the Report offers cost projections.

The great and the good, in the form of Georg Solti and Yehudi Menuhin, dealt glancing blows at the Report on the grounds that we were subjecting a noble art to the gruesome standards represented by the cash nexus. One can admire their commitment if not their logic, for it was an abrogation of responsibility for them to adopt the attitude that mundane questions about who shall pay for the intense pleasure that they give us should not sully any of their magisterial pronouncements. Clearly, neither had had time to read the Report. I wrote a letter (3 August 1970) in reply to a letter by Menuhin in *The Times* (25 July 1970) which pointed this out, and I must place on record that he sent me a personal letter graciously withdrawing the suggestion that we were trying to knock his profession and promising to read what we had said. It must also be added that Sir Georg later became one of the strong supporters of orchestral reform in London along the lines that we had suggested.

Perhaps the most honest and straightforward reaction to the Report came from the Musicians' Union, solidly lined up behind Hardie Ratcliffe, their chief official, and a member of the enquiry. The Report contains a Memorandum of Dissent by him (p. 47) for which he did not demand particular prominence. I must also add that he helped the enquiry in many practical ways and agreed with a large part of its analysis of the orchestral scene. What worried him and the MU was what was perceived to be the rejection of their wish to see orchestral employment expanded throughout Britain. Our refusal to propose an increase in the number of orchestras all round and to concentrate direct funding on two London orchestras seemed to be contrary to players' interests. I could argue the toss with him, as we did on several occasions, but here I only wish to say that however misconceived the arguments of the MU seemed to me, I respected them. They were certainly powerfully enough expressed and strong objections from the MU were certainly one of the reasons why the Arts Council, not always noted for its robustness towards clients, shrank from accepting so much of our Report.

REFLECTIONS

Reflecting on my buffeting from all and sundry as a result of the Report, I have to remember that 'battles long ago' may not be of much interest to readers other than those directly involved in the associated events. So let me try to extract a general observation about my experience which may help those likely to become engaged in similar exercises and placed in the firing line.

When my first book was published in 1952 I met an elderly female colleague at LSE who had heard that this was the day of its publication. She said: 'Don't be too disappointed. You no doubt woke up expecting that the world had changed but found that it was totally unaware of the fact. Moreover, don't expect anything to happen once your book has appeared'. It was good advice. The book, *The Economics of National Insurance*, was panned in a review in a professional journal by no less a person than the Warden of Nuffield College, Norman Chester. I was so upset (and so naive) that I phoned my publisher to apologise. He said: 'Wait a minute – did you say *Norman Chester*? How *long* was the review?' I told him 1,200 words. To my astonishment, he was delighted. The eminence of the reviewer and the length of the review were a measure of the book's importance – not the reviewer's adverse opinion!

I was therefore not entirely surprised that nothing seemed to happen after the Report had made its initial impact. However, it can fairly be claimed that, over the years, the argument of the Report has become the point of departure of discussion of some of the major policy issues surrounding the creation and performance of music, even amongst those who, for one reason or another, have rejected its conclusions. While this may offer some consolation to those who undergo similar experiences, one must face the fact that the originators of fresh ideas on policy questions are frequently forgotten and the ideas are presented by successive generations of pundits as if they were their own. If the ideas have any impact at all on actual policy measures, then it can be long after they were first promulgated. One must also accept that policy-making bodies rarely accept proposals in the round – our own were highly interdependent – but will 'cherrypick' their way through them, so it is advisable to be careful about assuming the credit for policy changes which are claimed to have been derived from one's intellectual efforts.

5

INTERMEZZO (2)
Eine Kleine Statistik

AN UNUSUAL AND WELCOME ALLY

One of many prominent musicians who gave evidence to the ORE was Professor Thurston Dart (1921–71), well known at the time as a keyboard specialist and musicologist who revolutionised appreciation of eighteenth-century music. For an amateur like myself his book *The Interpretation of Music* (1954) had been a revelation. What has been forgotten is that he was also a trained mathematician who had learnt operational research (OR) techniques during his war service. His evidence followed ideas about how OR could be used to analyse the orchestral situation which he had previously expressed in an article published in the *Musical Times* in 1965 with the intriguing title of 'Musical Dinosaurs and Operational Research'.

Operational Research, as used by the military, is a mathematical technique applied to deal with the identification of the ways in which scarce defence resources could be devoted to alternative uses, so as to maximise their effectiveness in achieving stated military objectives. In other words, the mathematicians had stumbled across the opportunity cost problem which I introduced in Chapter 3, and which economists were already trying to explain and interpret to Churchill's war cabinet. Operational Research gave quantitative expression to the economist's concept which tried to ensure that relevant data were collected and organised in a mathematical model. The model itself could be tested by using alternative assumptions about the relation between inputs of resources and the output of military effort, and had to be flexible enough to reveal the consequences of changing the mix of objectives as priorities changed.

In his article, Dart tried to market OR to his fellow-musicians by a three-stranded argument. First, he explained in simple language what OR was all about, rather as I have attempted to do in the last paragraph. He disarmed advance criticism by a carefully worded conclusion: 'OR works particularly well when we need to sort out and judge between conflicting claims . . . . At worst, it can too easily generate into time-and-motion study of the most inhuman kind. Properly used, however, there is no door that OR cannot unlock, no dilemma it cannot help resolve'.

Second, he emphasised that, like M. Jourdain in *Le Bourgeois gentilhomme* who spoke good prose without knowing it, we all unbeknowingly use OR techniques in planning our daily lives. We can aim to be at the office at a certain time. We have a model in our minds of the alternative means of transport, and how long it is likely to take by each means and how much it will cost. Our choice may be between minimising cost by walking, which, however, takes an hour, as against taking only twenty minutes by car but at greater cost in the form of petrol and parking charges. (This is my example not Dart's!)

Third, he illustrated his case by reference to the Goodman Report (see p. 55 above) which had clearly made him pretty angry. The Goodman Committee contained 'no composer . . . no statistician'. In his view, its Report did not clarify its objectives, completely ignored chamber orchestras as part of the musical resources, and forged no link between the financial resources (including those of the BBC, the Arts Council and the GLC) and how these might be effectively employed. He concluded that: 'if discussion on method is artificially withheld in such matters . . . recommendations may well have shallow roots and will almost certainly have unforeseen consequences'.

Of course, Dart had a particular axe to grind, being a stout ally of those who saw the symphony orchestra as a musical dinosaur which would die a natural death if not subject to a mercy killing by positive policy action. I am deeply sorry that he died shortly after the ORE Report appeared so that there was no chance to enlist his help in persuading funding bodies to take more interest in analytical and statistical techniques in helping to improve policy decision making. I would also like to have argued through with him his case against using symphony orchestras as the source of the smaller musical resources necessary for presenting the kind of music which he so clearly loved.

Dart was so obviously right. If a funding body is to make rational decisions regarding the allocation of limited resources, it must be clear in its objectives and must have information, other than casual empiricism, which enables it to judge the contribution of those in competition for the funds available. Of course, we have to be careful to define what is meant by rational, and I shall offer an explanation later why funding bodies tend to believe that fudging and muddling through in decision making have much to be said for them. Furthermore, we must not forget Dart's warning about the misuse of analytical techniques. Those employing them too often give hostages to fortune by not explaining what they are doing and why to those most likely to be affected by any findings. Nor are members of prestigious bodies generally noted for their grasp of even the simplest statistical concepts. In fact, in my experience, they would feel an instinctive sympathy with Winston Churchill's father, Lord Randolph Churchill, who, when confronted as Chancellor of the Exchequer with the decimal point, remarked that he had often wondered what that damned dot meant.

I can give some idea what Thurston Dart was driving at by my experiences in trying to follow up the work of the ORE by explaining how fairly simple statistical analysis of orchestral activity might be presented to policy makers. This analysis only deals with one part of OR analysis, namely the relationship between the input of resources and the 'output' of orchestral music. There are problems enough in trying to do this, quite apart from whether it is regarded as making sense to orchestral managements and funding bodies. In fact, I can anticipate my account of further close encounters with the arts establishment by saying that it has strongly resisted any form of statistical investigation unless it seemed to support foregone conclusions.

EINE KLEINE METHODOLOGIE
Preliminaries

In judging success of commercial enterprises familiar indicators such as the rate of return on capital employed or the movement in their share prices are commonly used, though nowadays in judging their success from a social point of view other factors such as their anti-pollution or labour relations record may be taken into account. Orchestras like many other cultural enterprises are normally not expected to make a profit without subsidy and have no shares quoted on the market, but some measure of their success must be used, explicitly or implicitly, if only in taking decisions (on the taxpayer's and ratepayer's behalf) about the rate of subsidy they are to receive.

Clearly, even with commercial enterprises, the measure of success will be subjective, depending on whether one is a shareholder, a manager, a consumer or a worker; but at least a measure such as profit is familiar and once defined can be quantified and compared over time. The problem of measuring success becomes much more difficult and more obviously subjective when attempts are made to use several measures in different units (e.g. profits measured in money and industrial relations measured in, say, working days lost), and to weight the different measures.

In cases where commercial criteria are not considered overriding, and orchestras are a good example, less familiar indicators of 'success' have to be sought. These indicators are sometimes known as 'social indicators' to denote that they cannot be or that it is inappropriate for them to be expressed in terms of money. At the same time, if they are to indicate, for example, how an orchestra is faring, they must be capable of being expressed in quantifiable form. In crude language, these indicators must measure 'output' in some sense. However, no 'output', however measured, can be produced without requiring resources – in the orchestral case highly skilled professionals – which could be used in other ways. To obtain some impression as to whether these resources are being used in a form which merits the support of the taxpayer or ratepayer or the private patron, social indicators analysis can extend its operations to the devising of appropriate measures of 'resource inputs'. By comparing the movements in output and input indicators through time some tangible evidence may be offered which operates at least as a check on whether the enterprise in question has carried out its intentions and how its performance compares with similar enterprises.

At the mention of 'social' or 'performance' indicators the more patrician members of Arts Councils reach for their guns. This is not entirely understandable for any reasonably intelligent person would see that the kind of decisions they have to take require at least a minimum of relevant information. The rather lordly way in which arts pundits spurn the use of helpful statistical tools could be taken as evidence of their lack of confidence in their own *ex cathedra* judgments. However, in case any reader has doubts about my own awareness of limitations, let me make these clear:

(a)   It may be considered distasteful to 'quantify the unquanti-fiable'. Enjoyment or satisfaction of individuals cannot be measured in easily identifiable units and one may resist the very idea of applying a calculus to the sublime moments one may have experienced in the concert hall. At the same time, ranking performances of an individual orchestra or comparing rankings of different orchestras take place all the time, even if precise forms of measurement may not be used. In a hard world where resources are limited there must be some quantitative base for the allocation of subsidies.

(b)   There must be argument about the choice of measures. That is agreed. Not only is the choice of measures arbitrary but the weights to be attached to each measure must also be arbitrary. What I have sought to do is to explore the implications of using some existing indicators, but in so doing I do not seek to influence the choices of anyone. The way of trading off one measure against another is designed only to explain how this might be done. It is the method of approach which may have general application, not the results. In particular no judgment is passed on the activities of any individual orchestra.

Activity Indicators

Let me begin by looking at 'output' (or, if you prefer, 'activity') in a familiar way. Two common measures are number of perfor-mances and number of seats sold (in total or per performance). It is not too difficult to get information about major orchestras for a series of years which would show the trend in output or activity. I illustrate our simple methodology by using 'performed output' rather than 'marketed output' (seats sold) for two reasons. The first is that if one wants to produce more sensitive indicators of activity, then this indicator is more easily modified. The second is that, given that one wants to compare activity with the costs of producing it, then there is a much more direct link between performances and working sessions generally (including rehearsal time) and costs. This is clearly demonstrated by the fact that if more seats are sold than expected, costs do not rise *pari passu* with the size of the audience.

By way of illustration, look at Table 5.1, which records the number of concert performances by a symphony orchestra over a period of eight years. (These are based on actual figures but I do not identify the orchestra.)

Hold on, you say. Every concert is different. The standard of play varies. The programme differs, with some concerts having more contemporary music than others. The audiences differ – some concerts serve educational purposes. The location differs, it being one thing to be playing 'at home' as distinct from 'away'. And so on. The output or activity is both intangible and variegated. Concerts are not homogeneous units. Of course, all that is true, but we might be able to refine our index. We can begin in a simple way by looking at the composition of concerts, as shown in Table 5.2. The categories used are again illustrative and certainly not exhaustive.

Now we come to the tricky stage. How do we weight the various activities in a sensible way so that we produce a more refined measure of activity? There are separate questions. The first is who is to do the weighting? The second is what weights to use? If the measure of activity is seats sold, then both questions can be answered very easily. The weights given to each activity are decided by the concert audience, and their subjective valuations of different sorts of concerts are reflected in their seat

TABLE 5.1: General Measure of Output or Activity of the Utopia Symphony Orchestra.

	Year							
	1	2	3	4	5	6	7	8
Number of concerts	135	154	163	150	159	162	156	154

purchases. In other words, provided that concert-goers have alternative forms of enjoyment available, either in the form of competing musical activities or substitutes in the form of other cultural activities, the box-office is a very sensitive indicator of audience choice and the weighting of different types of concert are automatically registered. Moreover, seats sold will register very quickly any *change* in weightings as between different orchestral 'products'.

It follows that the use of weights implies that audience choice as registered through seats sold is not regarded, by someone or some body, as an overriding criterion for judging the performance of an orchestra. Even an orchestra mindful of the box office and therefore sensitive to audience choice, might use weights which reflect 'job satisfaction' (e.g. *1812* only once a month), audience development, and prestige with fellow musicians and critics. The hard fact is, however, that weighting must be implicit in the judgments which are made by funders other than audiences, such as public grant-giving bodies and private sponsors, and their weightings will be of most practical interest. The hard bargains struck between such funding bodies and orchestras are all about weightings given to alternative orchestral activities though neither side, for strategic reasons, may wish to be too specific about their choice of weights.

It would be presumptuous of me to recommend what weights should be used and difficult for me to detect what are the implicit weights used by funding bodies either in the past or at present. What I can do is to show what happens to our activity measure if we take alternative sets of weights. Once

TABLE 5.2:   USO Concert Characteristics.

Concert type	Year							
	1	2	3	4	5	6	7	8
Total number	135	154	163	150	159	162	156	154
concerts	25	33	32	32	26	16	13	9
Educational concerts	18	18	18	18	22	21	15	11
Concerts with one new work	28	20	19	42	29	23	29	25
Concerts with two new works	9	12	23	8	6	10	4	9
Concerts with three new works	3	0	0	2	0	7	8	4
Concerts with 'local' music	2	0	0	17	12	6	6	10
'Out of Town' concerts	25	33	32	32	26	16	13	9

TABLE 5.3:   Weighting Systems.

Concert type	Weighting systems				
	0	A	B	C	D
Total number	1.0	1.0	1.0	1.0	1.0
'Out of Town' concerts	1.0	1.3	1.6	1.6	1.8
Educational concerts	1.0	1.4	1.7	1.7	2.0
Concerts with one new work	1.0	1.2	1.2	1.2	1.5
Concerts with two new works	1.0	1.3	1.3	1.3	1.7
Concerts with three new works	1.0	1.5	1.5	1.5	1.1
Concerts with 'local' music	1.0	1.5	1.6	1.7	1.5

TABLE 5.4:   Weighted Indicators of USO/activity.

	Weighting system				
Year	0	A	B	C	D
1	135.0	157.0	170.0	172.4	196.6
2	154.0	178.0	194.0	194.0	216.8
3	163.0	194.5	210.3	217.5	244.2
4	150.0	187.1	203.8	205.5	247.9
5	159.0	189.2	204.8	206.0	238.5
6	162.0	189.3	201.0	206.4	231.0
7	156.0	179.9	188.9	194.3	216.5
8	154.0	175.8	182.8	183.8	210.4

readers know how this is done, they can substitute their own weighting sets.

In Table 5.3, we present some arbitrary alternative weights. There are five systems, with '0' system being our unweighted system (see Table 5.1) and the remainder adding a weighing factor for the concert types listed in Table 5.2. Weighting system '0' contains a column of 1s reflecting equal weighting irrespective of type of activity. In all other systems, a concert counts for more than 1, if it is characterised by one of the factors listed in Table 5.2. Thus in weighting system B, an educational concert has a weighting of 1.7 and a concert with one new work one of 1.2. If we now multiply the weightings to the number of concerts under each heading in Table 5.2, as we show in Table 5.4, we are able to modify our crude measure in Table 5.1. It is apparent that the arbitrary weights increase the absolute value of output quite considerably, but, reading down the columns in Table 5.4, one notices that the trend value of output is not greatly altered.

The Cost of Orchestral Input

Orchestral managements as well as funding bodies are interested, of course, in what it costs to provide concerts, and how those costs vary per unit of activity in a particular year or over a period of years. The concept of cost which I use in this analysis is economic rather than financial cost, so let me explain the difference as simply as possible. The main point to be made is that financial cost is not the same as economic cost, and it is the latter that is relevant in comparing the orchestral input with output. This is because the cost of providing orchestral performances for our enjoyment should be measured in terms of the alternatives forgone in the form of other goods and services that could have been produced by the resources committed to these performances. In times of inflation financial cost is clearly a poor measure of the change in resources used, because it does not allow for changes in the value of money, or, more accurately, the changes in musicians' remuneration per session and other costs. Further, even if allowance is made for inflation and the financial cost readjusted for inflation is taken to represent the resources used in producing orchestral music which could be used to produce other things, it is being implicitly assumed that, if there were no orchestras, these resources would be fully employed in some alternative use. It is a moot point whether, if there were no government-supported orchestras, orchestral musicians would be absorbed into other forms of musical activity or other forms of employment, and the various concert halls in which they play would find alternative lettings.

I have adopted the not unreasonable assumption that the orchestral players in the USO could obtain alternative employment either in other orchestras or in other occupations so we value the alternative use of their talents by their salaries, after allowing for price changes. As there is a presumption that, with no USO concerts, concert halls in which they play would be under-utilised, I exclude payments by the USO for the use of concert halls from the cost estimates. Actually, while this lowers the economic cost below the financial cost figures, both adjusted for inflation, little difference is made to the *trend* in costs.

The Trend in Activity and Input

The final stage of this brief analysis requires us to compare the movements in the indices of activity or output with the movements in the index of costs. The usual reason for doing this in industrial studies is in order to estimate changes in productivity, though this is only one measure of productivity which might be used. Thus if an index of activity rises faster than the index of costs, productivity will have increased and vice versa.

Two preliminary comments may be made before examining the data. The first is that 'productivity' is used here only as a convenient shorthand expression and movements in the productivity indices, while perhaps of some interest, are not designed to pass a firm judgment on the management of orchestral affairs. The second is that 'productivity' must not be confused with 'efficiency'. Broadly speaking, the normal meaning of efficiency in economics involves a comparison between using resources in one way compared with another. If resources in existing employments produce less benefits than in alternative employments, then they are not used efficiently. Thus it is possible for productivity to decrease (i.e. benefits offered, however measured, rise at a slower rate than costs) yet resources may still be being used efficiently so long as the benefits produced by the alternative uses of the resources employed in the sector displaying declining productivity are estimated to be less. It will be noted that I have deliberately avoided any attempt to define how benefits from alternative employment of resources are to be identified and measured or whose definition of benefit is considered relevant. In Table 5.5 I express the absolute figures for activity in index form, taking the Year 1 figure in all cases as the base year i.e. Year 1 = 100. Alongside these indices, we place the associated index of economic cost. In this particular example, the index of economic cost rose by 24 per cent, but all the indices of activity rose by less than this percentage. There are ups and downs throughout this period, which act as a warning that conclusions from this kind of analysis may depend very much on the time period chosen. It is not the

TABLE 5.5:   Indices of Activity and Economic Cost.
              (Year 1 = 100)

Year	Economic cost	0	A	B	C	D
			Weighting systems			
1	100.0	100.0	100.0	100.0	100.0	100.0
2	87.5	114.1	113.4	114.1	112.5	110.3
3	119.5	120.7	123.9	123.7	126.2	124.2
4	125.2	111.1	119.2	119.9	119.2	126.1
5	121.2	117.8	120.5	120.5	119.5	121.3
6	119.6	120.0	120.6	118.2	119.7	117.5
7	122.8	115.6	114.6	111.2	112.7	110.1
8	124.0	114.1	112.0	107.5	106.6	107.0

statistician who 'lies with the statistics', but those who use them.

Presentation of Conclusions

Put yourself in the position in which I have frequently found myself in which you are asked to present an analysis of this kind to those unfamiliar with and possibly sceptical, even hostile to OR-type exercises. It is truly amazing how many inexperienced consultants there are who play their cards close to their chests and then reveal their findings at the end of their investigations to clients who are treated as if they were appearing before the inquisition, instead of conducting a continuing dialogue with those who have asked them for help. If you simply reported the results of this analysis to an orchestral client as showing that 'over eight years your productivity has fallen', you would not only be adding fuel to the fire of hostility but would be acting unscientifically. Worse still, your client is likely to refuse to send you the final instalment of your fee and even threaten to sue you for what has been paid out to you already. In explaining how a constructive dialogue might be entered into with a client, I believe one can demonstrate both the credibility and the versatility of the analytical approach which Thurston Dart tried to sell to his own profession.

The first obvious thing to do is to consult the client about the weighting system. If the client were the USO, then clearly it would derive more benefit from attaching its own weights to the special factors which we have outlined and might suggest other factors that it considered relevant. This must be done while the exercise is under way, if only to increase confidence in the methodology being used. The client might also be encouraged to test the weighting system for sensitivity by adopting a range of weightings for each factor. Of special interest might be the weights which the USO surmises as to be those which a government or other funding body might consider relevant.

The above example has been chosen deliberately because the result achieved, at first sight, suggests that the orchestra is not doing as well as it might. The process of dialogue means that this result would come as no surprise to the client, instead of being a shock to the system which causes the customary adverse reaction to the bringer of bad news. The consultant can be quite helpful in the interpretation of the results. (S)he can point out that all that the data mean is that more resources per concert were required later in the period than earlier. This is only 'bad news' if this was not the expectation of the client or of those who finance its activities. In that connection, if the data become known to funding bodies, who are likely to be comparing the client's performance with that of others, then, in justice, similar calculations should be done for similar orchestras receiving funding. It would also be worth investigating the extent to which the economic cost was within the control of the client. This is an illustrative but not an exhaustive list of 'tips' which the investigator may produce, the general point being that the orchestral management should not be caught out making rash statements about the volume and quality of activity which are not compatible with the data.

Of course, it may always be tempting for clients to try to induce the investigator to 'massage' the data, so that (s)he becomes a hired gun. As I have hinted above, and will exemplify, it is not unknown for public bodies to hire economists and statisticians as part of their strategy to persuade the government to improve their funding. Quite apart from any questions of professional ethics, I would regard this as inexpedient. There is always the risk that the massaging may be exposed. From the investigator's point of view, any 'lapse' in professional standards can lose him/her the respect of his/her peers and, in consequence, bring about both a loss of personal utility and limitation on future employment. In economist's jargon, this could degenerate into a two-person negative sum non-co-operative game!

RESULTS OF FIELDWORK

This relatively simple, perhaps pedestrian, analysis was developed by me and a young economist called Nick Baigent, during my first and rather short period as a member of the Scottish Arts Council (1972–3). We wrote two memoranda for the Music Committee who were far from unsympathetic to the method. It was encouraging, too, to find that such a distinguished and versatile composer as Thomas Wilson did not think that we would do incalculable harm if the work was pursued. It was not followed up, presumably because I had to resign from the SAC when I was seconded to the Department of Trade and Industry as its Chief Economic Adviser (1973–6). Instead, I prepared and published a separate study on the London orchestras which was published during my period in that office. Civil service rules did not prevent me from publishing non-economic studies of a non-controversial nature, so I joined the ranks of those much greater figures such as Robert Burns and Geoffrey Chaucer (both excisemen), Anthony Trollope (Post Office) and the poet and Heine-translator Humbert Wolfe (Ministry of Labour) in extra-official authorship. It helped to maintain my sanity during the period when, perforce, I had to advise Mr Tony Benn. I sent my study, with some trepidation, to the *Musical Times*, for its editor, Stanley Sadie, had had some hard things to say about the ORE. He sent me a cordial letter of acceptance and published it as it stood in the July 1976 number.

The general results of this study (for which my wife, Margaret, slaved away at preparation of the tables) shown in Table 5.6 and are very similar to those found in the 'unidentified' orchestra case above.

In the case of three of the four orchestras the productivity indices fall over the period chosen for investigation whereas those of the Royal Philharmonic Orchestra both rise. Here we have a clear case where further investigation of the data would be necessary before any conclusions could be drawn. In the case of the RPO, we find that the base year 1966–67 was one in which performances and box office receipts were unusually low. If we take a different base year, e.g. 1969–70, the results are quite

TABLE 5.6: Notional Productivity Indices.
(1966–7 = 100)

Orchestra		1966–7	1967–8	1968–9	1969–70	1970–1	1971–2	1972–3	1973–4	1974–5
London Philharmonic Orchestra	A	100.0	96.4	91.9	94.0	95.8	100.2	91.9	93.3	96.7
	B	100.0	92.6	91.1	84.5	97.0	102.9	67.2	85.2	88.6
London Symphony Orchestra	A	100.0	93.9	103.4	93.0	97.1	94.2	100.7	97.4	95.6
	B	100.0	102.2	52.8	64.1	74.5	59.6	77.2	73.5	65.5
New Philharmonia Orchestra	A	100.0	91.7	85.8	89.4	90.2	105.3	106.7	100.3	82.9
	B	100.0	77.1	65.3	90.8	89.0	86.4	116.3	89.1	82.1
Royal Philharmonic Orchestra	A	100.0	87.3	87.1	79.5	88.9	85.3	88.5	82.7	107.1
	B	100.0	98.1	120.8	101.2	115.4	142.1	103.7	145.8	175.1

A: Index of performances/Index of costs × 100
B: Index of total seats sold/Index of costs × 100

different – the reader can check for him/herself. It was possible to make some allowance for 'quality' in output by putting in weights for the percentage of performances of works of living composers and for the ratio of rehearsal time to performances, but these made no substantial difference to the results.

This study did not excite any comment from musical pundits, which is perhaps not surprising, but formed part of a growing collection of studies which sought to discover the prevalence of 'Baumol's disease' (Chapter 2). The real growth in orchestral costs, i.e. after allowing for inflation, was clearly quite substantial in the 1960s and early 1970s, and very much in line with the growth in input costs in the economy as a whole. With no productivity gains and no major changes in the balance of programmes, orchestras survived by raising their ticket prices faster than the rate of inflation, although there was a small increase in the relative importance of government subsidies.

However, the musical world, including opera, woke up, after the oil crisis in 1973, to the fact that a relative increase in costs could not be absorbed by increasing ticket prices above the level of inflation and by a larger proportion of subsidy income to music companies, during a period when the government was trying to cut down the rapid rate of inflation by controlling the rate of growth in personal incomes and by more rigid control of government expenditure. However, one way out of the difficulty could be found if it could be shown that in periods of rapid inflation, as occurred in the 1970s, the performing arts, including orchestras and opera, were more adversely affected than other sectors through factors beyond their control. Knowing of my continuing interest in the economics of orchestral activity and of my previous membership of the SAC, the ACGB commissioned me to measure the effect of inflation on the performing arts (see Peacock, Shoesmith and Milner, 1983). The clear expectation was that our detailed study would back the hunch that inflation hit the arts harder than other government-financed sectors and this would strengthen the case for preserving the real level of subsidies for the performing arts in particular.

I realised pretty soon after the study was begun that I was likely to be in trouble once again. My good friend of many years, Claus Moser, then head of the Government Statistical Service, was on record as saying that 'Inflation tends to hit artistic institutions harder than ordinary industrial or commercial enterprises. Wages and salaries account for a very high proportion of expenditure . . . and the scope to offset cost increases by improvements in productivity is strictly limited and by now nearly exhausted' (Moser, 1981).

He spearheaded a public campaign to have these facts recognised. It was not immediately obvious to me why there need be any connection between Baumol's 'cost disease' based on the labour intensity of the performing arts and being at a disadvantage because of inflation. There was no *a priori* reason why in a period of rapid inflation, such as that being experienced in the 1970s and early 1980s, the proportion of wage and salary costs should be the deciding factor in determining why arts companies should be at a differential disadvantage. Input costs of raw materials, particularly of imports, might rise just as rapidly as wage costs. During the oil crisis, clearly fuel-intensive industries would be more adversely affected by the enormous rise in oil prices. There was even evidence that one might reach the opposite conclusion for we soon found out that in the period 1972–80 wage costs in manufacturing industry rose about three times, whereas costs of materials and fuels rose four and a half times.

Whatever doubts Eddie Shoesmith, Geoff Milner and I – all members of the staff of the then highly controversial institution, the University College at Buckingham – might have had about the hypothesis, it could hardly be denied that we knew how to conduct a thoroughly professional empirical investigation. (Ironically, Eddie had been a much respected member of Claus's staff shortly before this.) But there was a further difficulty. Apart from knotty conceptual and technical problems, would the data be available? I may have misled the reader into thinking that the data so far presented was easily come by, but this was not so. The data on orchestras as not perfect, but it was adequate. The reason for that was that a condition of subsidy in the London orchestras was the provision of such data to the London Orchestral Concerts Board; in short it was a by-product of the administrative process. It might have been thought that the provision of subsidies by the ACGB and by local authorities would have made statistical collection a matter of assimilating data available in their records, but this was far from being the case, which is itself an interesting commentary on their appraisal and monitoring procedures. One can sympathise with grant-giving bodies faced with this problem. Arts organisations can appear and disappear very rapidly; their standard of accounting and reporting at this time varied enormously (and this was not necessarily a function of their size and reputation); their ability and willingness to have their records made available to even an ACGB-sponsored researcher would vary according to the perceived benefits which might follow from co-operation. There was nothing for it but to take a sample of companies and to study their accounts in depth. We did in fact obtain some reasonably reliable data, entirely due to our fortunate choice of three married women economists as researchers – Anna Campbell MacLean, Kathleen Rennie and Ruth Towse – whose charm and persistence helped to remove formidable communication barriers with our subject matter.

The study took two years and has been widely recognised as a major contribution to statistical analysis of the arts, a claim I can fairly make because the detailed professional statistical work is entirely due to Eddie Shoesmith and Geoff Milner. My contribution was to extract the economics conclusions from their evidence, subject to their useful criticism. There was a deathly hush when it reached the desks of senior officials at the ACGB. No professional criticism was received, but then the ACGB's Finance Director, Tony Field, and Statistical Officer, George Darroch, had been kept fully informed about our progress and were nothing if not helpful. The only text I was asked to alter was the title, at the request of the Deputy Secretary General, Richard Pulsford, whose Treasury background no doubt made him acutely aware of solecisms. (Things are not the same at the Treasury now, I suspect, having recently seen one of their memos, where 'principle' is used instead of 'principal'.) He was quite right, of course, in pointing out that it is a violation of grammar to talk about the 'performing' instead of the 'performed' arts, though we were following the rest of the world's practice which, regrettably, Mr Pulsford has failed to have eradicated.

The reader has probably guessed that, once again, an unwelcome result was forthcoming. Our carefully detailed researches showed, quite unequivocally, that the differential effect of inflation on the performing – sorry – performed – arts over the period in question (1970–82) was comparatively slight. The reader interested in the details should consult the Report itself (Peacock,

Shoesmith and Milner, 1983), but all that need be said here is that, in the case of the London orchestras alone, the average annual change in real costs (after allowing for inflation), actually fell throughout the 1970s and early 1980s and, correspondingly, the index of costs – whichever statistical method is chosen – rose at a somewhat slower rate than the Retail Price Index as a general index. Any case for increasing public subsidies to arts organisations solely because of differential inflation effects was destroyed. I am told that the ACGB were very taken aback and horror was expressed at the 'enormous' cost of the study itself. The Chairman is alleged to have remarked that the survey 'would have been cheap at the price, if it had come to the right conclusion'. I was not told at the time that the ACGB had sent the study to Will Baumol in the expectation that he might find something wrong with it, but apparently he didn't! At least this time the Report was published without a disclaimer – but, alongside the usual glossy productions of that institution, it has a pathetic look, being 'published' by simply photocopying the typescript.

RITORNELLO

This further close encounter with the world of music displays once again two recurring themes in my discourse. Musicians behave like other people when faced with similar constraints on their actions. Evaluating their services to the community by means other than direct payments to them made by those who enjoy their performances is remarkably difficult.

The fact that orchestral costs per session had risen less than costs in general could only mean that in the 1970s and early 1980s orchestral players had taken a cut in their earnings relative to other occupations. In fact, players' fees relative to wage rates in other professional employments had decreased, and playing sessions were reduced, largely by a reduction in the ratio of rehearsal to performance time. Usually in conditions of inflation, well organised professional unions will try and often succeed in inducing employers to pass wage claims forward onto consumers so that their traditional differentials with other professional unions are maintained. If, as in the 1970s, inflation was combined with meagre increases in economic growth, unions would still seek to maintain the real value of wages, even if this meant the risk of unemployment amongst its members. Why did this not happen in the case of orchestral players?

The answer lies in the rational response of the orchestral players to their economic situation. They had no expectations that wage claims could be passed on in the form of higher seat prices if that were to result in a fall in the number of seats sold. That the ACGB or local authorities would increase their funding to compensate for any shortfall in box-office receipts did not seem in prospect. However, the striking difference with other professional groups faced with a similar financial situation lay in the lack of the 'shedding labour option' as a means of maintaining their relative position in the wages and salary hierarchy. The inflexible nature of the orchestral repertoire meant that firing the last two desks of all string sections and the fourth member of every woodwind and brass section would destroy the product and put a whole orchestra out of business. That is clearly in no-one's interests.

No matter how hard one presses the point that statistical analysis is only a tool and that those who prepare and present it should have no other purpose in mind than to provide useful information which might otherwise remain undiscovered, it is only human to distrust the things that we do not understand. The illustrations used in this chapter, which accord with the proposals of such a distinguished musician as Thurston Dart, are designed to how careful one must be in monitoring the quality of data, analysing and presenting it in intelligible form and that one must be particularly careful in its interpretation.

In the last analysis, the reader is entitled to question whether attempts to measure the degree of success of any artistic institution is worth the effort. An answer to this question can only be given by asking him/her to answer the more fundamental question: by whom and by what method should the relative size of the performing arts, music included, be decided? If one believes that the sole arbiters of the value of music should be those who enjoy and pay for it, either through the box-office or by other voluntary means, e.g. as donors, elaborate statistical measures of performance may not seem necessary. Voluntary payment for musical services rendered is a very sensitive indicator of consumer and donor preferences. Of course, the formation and fulfilment of such preferences depends on accurate information about alternative sources of musical enjoyment. If payers are to rely on the guidance sought from educators, critics and musicians themselves, then their mentors will give them better service if their assessments have some better foundation than reliance on their authority. If the reader is sceptical of the efficiency of the market as an allocator of resources for music, and believes in public support for the arts, then (s)he has the right to expect that the amount and form of that support can be justified by reference to explicit and publicly-known criteria which can be given some form of quantitative expression.

6

MOTO PERPETUO
Composers of the World Unite

About twenty years ago, I was invited to and enjoyed a particularly good lunch given by a music publisher of some eminence, indeed notoriety. It was the first occasion that I had met him – and the last – we never met again. In typical British fashion it began with a rather formal handshake and predictable observations on the weather, with the dialogue moving gradually towards identifying those acquaintances we had in common and how we had come across them. The aperitifs performed miracles in destroying any remaining barriers in the way of communication and, as the wine flowed, so did the conversation. Perhaps it was less of a conversation and rather a marvellous off-the-record disquisition on the delights and perils of music publishing punctuated by my almost uncontrollable laughter. My only worry was how I would ever remember some of the splendid asides on problems of musical copyright, the subject which had brought us together. By the main course we were great buddies, and caused something of a mild sensation as we left the restaurant offering a close harmony rendition of some music hall song, possibly 'Nellie Dean'. No-one should be surprised that I cannot remember whether it was or not.

What I do remember is that, as we walked down Regent Street, my host suddenly stopped as an ambulance scattered the traffic and uttered its familiar ominous, jarring, two-note fanfare. He shouted in my ear: 'Jesus, I wish I owned the copyright of that tune!' Of course, claiming copyright to a tune of repeated minor thirds – we were not sure whether a minor third or major second in our convulsed state – would be a nonsense. Before we parted at the bottom of the street, near the Cafe Royal, we had identified about twelve themes that began with a minor third, from the extremes of 'Colonel Bogey' to the Quartet from the first act of *Fidelio*. But the incident brought into clear focus the problems encountered by composers in making a living. I touched on these problems in Chapters 2 and 3, but my meeting with the jolly publisher concerned very practical issues with which I became deeply involved in the 1970s and then again many years later.

Imagine that you are a composer who is walking down Regent Street and you hear an ice-cream van – not an ambulance – blaring forth one of your melodies in order to attract custom. By what steps could you ensure that you would be paid for your services?

Step 1: You would have to register the work, usually through a publisher, as your copyright.

Step 2: You would have to make it available in a form in which it can be played. Normally this would mean that the work would be available as sheet music or, more common nowadays, on tape.

Step 3: You or someone would have to negotiate the terms on which the work could be performed.

Step 4: You would have to find some means for detecting when and in what form the work is being performed. (Someone might hear your work performed 'live' and make a recording for putting on disc for 'pirate' sale.)

Step 5: You would have to ascertain whether or not you were legally entitled to payment if the work is publicly performed, in whole or in part.

Step 6: If your rights are infringed, seeking redress may require you to take legal action, involving time and money.

The opportunity cost to the individual composer of trying single-handed to enforce his/her rights is clearly very high. But things have progressed since the days when Beethoven had to put an advertisement in the press to announce that the only correct copies of his works could be found with Breitkopf and Härtel in Leipzig. This was his only defence against pirated editions which at the time could not be legally prevented. The establishment of more stringent copyright laws in the nineteenth century coupled with better communications paved the way for composers to appoint 'agents' to exploit these rights. Among the most famous has been and is the British Performing Right Society who called on me to advise them on a particularly difficult matter. Indeed, it was in the course of this advice-giving that I had reason to meet the jolly publisher who was a member of the Society's Council.

It will be clear to any expert on intellectual copyright that my description of the composer's problem of extracting payment from users of his product is highly simplified, to say the very least. However, in order to demonstrate why a knowledge of economics seemed to have been helpful in this instance, it is fortunately not necessary for me to burden the reader with recondite matters of law. What I have to explain briefly is how the PRS operates and how it was that they called on me to help them.

'GIVING MUSIC ITS DUE'

The Performing Right Society (PRS) was founded in 1914 in response to the Copyright Act of 1911 whose relevant provisions made copyright infringement a criminal offence and entitled the composer to copyright protection for 'original work' for life plus a period of fifty years after his/her death. While, with certain important exceptions, the composer could not prevent 'performance' of his/her work, (s)he was entitled to collect payment for the performance. The words 'original work' and 'performance' are in inverted commas because it must already be apparent that definitions of such terms must be a complex matter. It is important for my narrative to know that it was early established that 'performance' extended to 'canned' as well as 'live' performance, notably through radio and latterly television broadcasting.

Clearly, the only way that individual composers could take advantage of the legislative provisions, which have been subject to periodical review and alteration to take account of techno-logical and institutional changes, was to join forces. From small beginnings, the PRS has become a dominant force in promoting and extending the economic interests, not only of composers but also of publishers and lyric writers.

A brief idea of its complicated task is also necessary as a prelude to the account of my involvement in the PRS's affairs:

(a)   It negotiates royalty payments for composers collectively and distributes receipts amongst them broadly according to the use made of individual composers' works.

(b)   It identifies the various classes of user in negotiating royalties, with the result that there are over forty separate tariffs. These cover public performance, including pubs (juke boxes), discotheques, cinemas and airlines, BBC and independent radio and television broadcasting and latterly cable and satellite stations.

(c)   Typically it grants a blanket licence to a class of user who can then 'perform' any item in the PRS repertoire.

(d)   It has a policing system (a team of inspectors) to safeguard against unlawful use of copyright music. (Punch-ups have been known to take place in pubs where inspectors have discovered that tenants do not hold a juke box licence.)

(e)   In order to ensure equitable division of royalties as well as to collect data relevant to tariff negotiations, it monitors performance programmes extensively. For example, broadcasting stations send complete returns of all music used and the PRS monitors broadcasting programmes on a sampling basis as a check on the accuracy of returns. Administrative expenses are therefore not a negligible item of PRS expenditure (they equal about 12 per cent of total revenue) and will vary considerably as between particular classes of user.

(f)   It acts as a collecting agency for overseas-based composers, with an international link-up with similar societies in other countries which collect royalties for British-based composers.

(g)   Typically, it negotiates with groups of users, and not with individuals, and some of these groups are powerful and well organised.

A final preliminary point concerns membership of the PRS. There are two main categories: composers and lyricists, and publishers. The composers and lyricists can become provisional members relatively easily on the basis of a small number of professional performances of their work whereas publishers must have a minimum catalogue of works. They graduate to associate and then to full membership on the basis of a minimum level of royalties collected on their behalf. Full membership carries the right to nominate or be nominated to membership of the governing body – the Council – which consists of an equal number of composers/lyricists and publishers. The Council appoints an Executive which operates rather like the board of directors of a company and is responsible for the management of the society's affairs.

This description of the PRS has conjured up the picture of a composers' co-operative which could exercise its monopoly power to the detriment of music users. It is true that economies of scale in royalty collection are large so that it would be very difficult, at least in a country the size of the UK, to imagine that it would be in anyone's interests to set up in competition. However, although there might not be any intention to prevent other organisations competing in the collection business, the fact that the origin of the monopoly lay in technical rather than institutional factors has no bearing on whether or not monopoly power is exploited. Broadly speaking music users, claiming that they represent the audience at large at one remove, have not questioned the principle of property rights in artistic creation and, indeed, in performance. What they have questioned is both the attempts to extend the definition of performance and the freedom of the PRS and other collecting agencies collecting revenue from 'mechanical performance' to charge what they like.

Two examples from the history of the PRS's relations with users illustrate this point. As early as the 1970s the PRS members were worried at the effect of the technological changes which led to the very substantial improvement in the quality of taping of live and 'canned' performance, including video-recording of TV programmes of copyrighted work, and also the growing availability of inexpensive recording equipment. Recording for home use was clearly against the interest of PRS members and, indeed, it was certainly within the spirit of copyright legislation that composers should be compensated for the 'do-it-yourself' performance system. In my view, prevention of home taping would be both impracticable and undesirable, and I had the opportunity of expressing this view to the PRS in the course of the reports that I wrote for them which I consider in more detail below. It seemed to me that the public should be entitled to record and that, rather than obtain a royalty payment indirectly by a levy on recorders, the royalty should be based on use, which could be crudely measured by the number of tapes sold.

Discussion went on for some years, and the principle of charging for home recording by a levy on tapes was recommended by Mr Justice Whitford in a well known report, *Copyright and Designs Law* (HMSO, 1977), though I cannot claim that he derived the idea from my submission to him. A government Green Paper in 1985 threw the matter open for public discussion. It is easy to identify in advance who would be for and against the idea. I can do no better than quote from the summary of the debate in the Department of Trade and Industry's report on *Intellectual Property and Innovation* presented to Parliament in advance of proposed legislation in April 1986 (HMSO, 1986):

> The principle of a levy on audio tape was supported by the audio copyright interests and performers' organisations, the latter arguing that since home recording seriously affects the interests of performers, the performer concerned should be included among the beneficiaries of the levy proceeds, as they are in all of the countries which have already introduced a levy. Representatives of blind people and 'talking newspapers' voiced strong opposition and sought exemption from the levy . . . . Tape users who record non-copyright material, ranging from individuals to churches and small businesses, also expressed concern at the rough justice involved in their having to pay a levy. On video there was general resistance to payment of a levy in respect of 'time-shifting' (the main use of video tape) since it was felt the copyright interests had already been paid for the original broadcast. The film and other copyright interests, particularly those making training films and videos, were strongly against giving an entitlement to make private recordings directly from pre-recorded material, with or without a levy. A levy of any kind was strongly opposed by the manufacturers and importers of recording tape and equipment and by consumer organisations. (pp. 37–8)

The Department of Trade and Industry stated in the same document that the government had concluded that there was no realistic alternative to a compulsory levy on blank recording tape and that any levy scheme should give the public an entitlement to record for private purposes. Despite this statement, the government reversed engines and deleted any reference to the levy in the Copyright Designs and Patents Bill presented to Parliament in 1988, though it was defeated on this issue at the committee stage. The government responded by 'whipping in' support for non-inclusion and the Bill became the Act which bears its name. It is an open question why the government refused to support the levy, but some say that it was concerned about the political consequences of taxing a consuming pleasure of the young about to vote for the first time!

The second example goes back a bit in time to the days when the highly successful efforts of the PRS to recruit composers had led to the inevitable reaction amongst users of their music concerned about having to pay them. In the 1920s various attempts were made by users to exercise countervailing power, the more successful organisation being the International Council of Music Users Ltd. The ICMU sponsored a Bill to amend the Copyright Act of 1911. Two substantial amendments were proposed. The first was intended to make it compulsory to print a notice reserving the copyright on the performing right on every copy of the work as a condition for the retention of that right. It was the second that aroused the anger of composers. Its effect meant that if anyone bought a copy of sheet music, then he had the right to perform it by paying a fixed royalty of 2d for every copy bought. This fee covered the right in perpetuity to perform the work irrespective of the nature of the work, the place or manner of performance and the number of times performed. The so-called Tuppenny Bill assumed that the increase in the demand for music could be measured solely by sheet music sales which was patently absurd, particularly in days when radio broadcasting had led to an expansion in the number of wireless licences from about 36,000 in 1922 to over 2 million by 1926. By 1930, broadcasting royalties payable by the BBC had risen to £60,000, whereas the Bill would have allowed the BBC to broadcast any piece of music bought at 2d per copy. Thanks to a superb campaign spearheaded by, amongst others, A. P. Herbert, the Bill did not succeed, though it did lead to the setting up of a House of Commons Select Committee to examine the problem. It was the deliberations of that committee which led to a recommendation which subsequently resulted in the establishment of the Performing Right Tribunal (PRT) – an official body to resolve disputes over performance royalty questions. We shall hear more about it shortly.

It would be wrong to give the impression that the PRS from its inception had monopoly power which, if abused, would exploit a variety of users, from amateur musical societies to the orchestras of posh London hotels, who clearly would incur considerable costs in any attempt to exercise countervailing power. The position of the use was complicated by the importance of the BBC as a music user. Live musical performances began to take up a major proportion of broadcasting time, and there was intense controversy, which has lasted to the present day, as to whether broadcasting helped to publicize the composers' work or whether it reduced the audiences for live concert performances. In the end, with government approval, the BBC accepted that it should pay performance royalties, using the number of wireless licences as an indicator of music use. Some complicated legal issues arose, which need not detain us, though one interesting example which led to legal action by the PRS against a hotel chain concerned the relaying of broadcasts to hotel guests in a hotel lounge. Did this constitute performance? The case was decided in favour of the PRS.

It was the difference made by the BBC as a major factor in the market for musical composition which led to my involvement with the economics of copyright. It is perhaps not generally realised that only fifteen years after the establishment of the PRS, the BBC had become its most important individual customer providing no less than 35 per cent of the revenue from performing royalties by 1930. I mentioned that the absolute sum from this source in 1930 was £60,000. By the time I became involved in the early 1970s, this figure had risen to nearly £3m., representing 28 per cent of total royalties. (What had happened in the interim was that income from foreign affiliates had grown even more rapidly.) So a bi-lateral monopoly situation had arisen between the PRS and BBC, a situation which economists recognise as often unstable.

A DIGRESSION ON CONSULTANCY

Nobody raises an eyebrow in universities when economists accept consulting assignments for commercial concerns, international agencies and governments and are paid. The important proviso must be that anyone engaged in such work should give an undertaking to the university, his/her principal employer, that they will fulfil their teaching and research obligations notwithstanding any such assignment or must come to some arrangement satisfactory to colleagues and administration such as taking unpaid leave or turning over some or all of the proceeds of payment made to the university. Practice varies with the institution and the nature of the outside work. What is clear is that involvement in outside consultancy has become respectable because universities are anxious to show that those who teach can also practice. Besides, if academic salary scales are not flexible enough to take account of the detachability of staff of the highest quality who may be lured away, allowing them to make what it is hoped is an honest penny or two is one way of retaining them.

In my salad days as an economist at the LSE, I was lucky enough to be in an institution which took a relaxed view about outside work. That paragon amongst academic administrators, Alexander Carr-Saunders, simply required two assurances – that the arrangement was acceptable to colleagues if leave had to be taken and that the assignment was complementary to one's academic duties. One of my first jobs of this kind was to spend three weeks at the UN HQ in New York working on some fiscal policy problems which fitted well with my duties as Reader in Public Finance at the LSE. In my first encounter with an international bureaucrat in the UN finance section, I was floored by the following question: 'Are you with us as an expert or as a consultant?'. I had to confess I was unaware of my status and enquired what the difference was. 'Consultants are paid more' was the laconic reply. From that day on I have never claimed to be an expert.

In 1967 five economists headed by Victor Morgan and including John Dunning, Dennis Lees, Jack Wiseman and myself – all Professors of Economics at that time – set up an independent consultancy partnership. Even though we cleared the arrangement with our universities, we were rather concerned at colleagues' reactions. About this time there had been a cause célèbre in London University. That commanding figure in our profession, Lionel Robbins, had agreed to become the part-time Chairman of the *Financial Times*, with the blessing of the LSE Governors. The then Vice-Chancellor of the University of London made violent objection and mounted a campaign which drove Robbins from his Chair in Economics which he had held since 1932 and which he had filled with immense distinction. It was perhaps a rationalisation to claim that all the work we would undertake would be applied research, but there is no doubt that much of it was, and, moreover, survival in a highly competitive business meant high standards of output and, more difficult for academics, close attention to delivery dates.

I can only remember one colleague who sought to make an issue of outside earnings, and was preparing a memo for the Vice-Chancellor recommending that such earnings should be declared and also be subject to an upper limit. In conversation with the lady in question – a bureaucrat – I remarked that I had no objection to disclosure to the Vice-Chancellor but thought earnings limitations might be impracticable. Consistency would demand, however, that unearned income of colleagues should also be disclosed for, after all, those with a substantial amount of capital presumably spent valuable time considering their portfolio. 'Oh, yes', she replied. We heard no more on the matter.

I did not take a major part in the work of the Economists Advisory Group (EAG) as we called ourselves when it first began; and most of what I did was desk work. That was until the PRS approached me, having come across the Orchestral Resources Enquiry, about an ongoing dispute with the BBC which had already been considered by the Performing Right Tribunal. By that time the EAG was well equipped to undertake what promised to be a fascinating assignment. I can say at the outset that with Michael Freegard, still Chief Executive of the PRS, Denis de Freitas, then Legal Advisor of the PRS and a well known authority on copyright problems, and Marshall Lees, their economist who had attended my lectures at the LSE, rapport was easily established.

As often happens, it took some time to establish broad terms of reference. The lack of experience in dealing with economic consultants and, indeed, the lack of experience of academic consultants themselves in dealing with clients, meant that some time had to be spent on deciding where the comparative advantage of the EAG lay in clarifying the issues of the dispute before one could approach a position where sensible advice could be given. As it turned out, it was fortunate that it was early discovered that if we were to analyse the economic position of PRS members, then this would call for close and continuous contact with PRS staff at different levels and with several of its council members. Each side would be aware of how the project was progressing, which helped to build up confidence, and any surprising results from the work could be dealt with as these arose.

The terms of reference eventually agreed required me to organise a historical survey and statistical analysis of composers' earnings and then to consider whether this information could be used to present a case to the Tribunal which would enable that body to decide whether or not the formula of payment by the BBC for composers' performance rights was 'equitable'.

I have already (in Chapter 3) offered a few of the 'stylised facts' about composers' economic position and these are elaborated in my joint book with Ron Weir, *The Composer in the Market Place* (1975) which Donald Mitchell, later Chairman of the PRS and one of our best-known musicologists, published through Faber Music Ltd. I particularly enjoyed my association with him, which greatly increased my appreciation of the work of Mahler and Britten as well as allowing me to exploit to the full his remarkable knowledge of the economic position of the modern composer. A later work by Cyril Ehrlich commissioned by the PRS, *Harmonious Alliance* (1989), builds on our pioneering work but, curiously enough, makes scant reference to us. While essential background to the consulting work, the task itself called for statistical and analytical skills rather than those of the professional historian.

THE COMPOSERS' MITE

We began with a survey of composers' earnings, 'we' being Janet Cubitt, then a Research Fellow at York with an interest in music, and myself. The PRS had agreed to send a questionnaire to every one of the 2,873 British composers on its books as of September 1971, it being agreed, of course, that the earnings of no individual composer would be revealed. The then President of the PRS, the internationally known composer Sir Arthur Bliss, was enlisted to try to increase the response rate, and he wrote a persuasive letter to all those approached for information.

We were advised that a response rate of 33 per cent would be about par for such a survey; in actual fact it was 38 per cent. However, the response rate differed by composer category, it then being the practice that composers were 'serious' or 'light' or 'popular'. Two problems emerged in using the 1,084 replies. The response rate differed by category and not all composers could be classified. In the end we concentrated attention on tabulating results from 575 replies which could be classified in the required manner and which took account of the response rate.

It is tempting with such statistical investigation to correlate everything with everything else – how many red-haired composers write light music with their left hand? My narrative does not require presentation of such elaborations, interesting though they may be, for what is apposite is the PRS's reaction to our main findings. They did not seem to find it surprising that composers earned on average about £3,000 a year (about £11,000 at 1992 prices) from all sources and that there was little variation in this amount by category. Nor was it surprising to them that PR royalties represented only 16.4 per cent of the average earnings of 'pop' composers, 24 per cent for 'serious' and 33 per cent for 'light' composers. They had learnt something from us about the differences in sources of earnings. Not surprisingly 'pop' musicians made more from performing than from royalty income and earned more than a quarter of their income from non-musical activities. 'Serious' composers earned on average over one-third of their income from teaching, whereas 'light' composers tended, like their 'pop' counterparts, to go for performing.

Their publisher members accepted it as a sign of the times that sheet music earnings for all categories were negligible. Their position was well put by Ernst Roth in his splendid book, *The Business of Music*:

> Gone are the days when, at Christmas, music-publishers issued splendid volumes beautifully bound in linen or leather which were favourite gifts. In music-publishing Christmas now passes unnoticed, and records have taken the place of printed music. If the music-publisher, whether serious or popular, still had the dignified composure which he once shared with the book-publisher, simply selling music and leaving it to its fate, both he and his composers would end up in the workhouse. (pp. 86–7)

The publisher has now to go out into the highways and byways to promote orchestral performances which may sell a few orchestral parts but are more likely to require him to settle for hiring of parts, and may lead to interest being expressed by record companies in the works in question.

However, two things appeared to worry the PRS Council. The first was the 'skewness' in the distribution of earnings from PR royalties. A large proportion of composers in all categories earned less than £200 from PR royalties, with three-quarters of all serious composers alone falling into this class interval. In all categories upwards of 80 per cent of composers earned less than £1,000. At the other end of the royalty scale, approaching 10 per cent of light composers earned £2,000 or more but in the other categories the equivalent percentage was between 5 and 6 per cent. We knew from independent calculations that about 25 per cent of this small group were earning royalties of £20,000 or more. Looking at the dispersion of earnings by age group, the results were more intriguing than enlightening. The age group 41–50 recorded the highest average income by age of any category of composer, but this certainly reflected a very wide dispersion of earnings within this age group, with a handful of composers doing extremely well. This category also derived the greater part of its earnings from musical activities. In all categories, total earnings dropped dramatically in the age group 61+, which contained the largest proportion of composers. Earnings, however, are not synonymous with income and those in retirement, particularly if they had held teaching appointments or had been permanent employees, could be drawing an occupational pension in addition to a state National Insurance pension. The interesting question raised by this study of income by age was whether it would offer a picture of the prospective lifetime earnings which a composer might expect. We had to answer 'no'. The dispersion of earnings within each age group was considerable and it would be difficult for an individual composer on the threshold of his/her career to estimate the probability as to where they might land up within that dispersion. Furthermore, at the time of writing, the supply and demand conditions in the market for musical composition were undergoing considerable changes. A widely held expectation at the time of our enquiry was that a common interest in electronics coupled with the democratisation of taste would soon make it impossible to distinguish between one category of composer and another and between traditional composition and the development of electronic skills.

The second worrying item was presented by the analysis of the replies to the questions 'would you prefer to earn a larger proportion of your income from composing?', and 'if the . . . answer is "yes" briefly what do you see as the main obstacle to achieving your object?' The answer to the first question was generally 'yes', but the answers to the second brought forth what can only be described as a gorgeous collective bellyache. I should have expected this, because I know of no professional group who, when asked a question of this kind, would answer other than in terms that they are totally dissatisfied with their conditions of work and others are to blame for this! The difference was that the individual answers were nothing if not colourful, with only a handful prepared to state that their music was no longer fashionable or that inspiration had dried up. Leaving aside one or two replies which saw the main obstacle as racial prejudice, more disturbing was the picking on the BBC as the villain of the piece. It was certainly not in the interests of the PRS to conduct any negotiations with that body in an atmosphere of recrimination resulting from the perceptions of some alienated composers. I did take considerable trouble in seeking the observations of several musicians well versed in the difficulties that arise when one organisation, the BBC, was and is such a powerful influence on the fortunes of composers. No common view emerged. There were those who trusted the BBC to play fair and not to be captured by any one professional view of what was good pop, serious or light music. There were those who admitted that the BBC could never be perceived to get it right but that they seemed to have a prejudice against British music. And there were those who were downright hostile and based their hostility on the alleged ignorance of the music scene. As one colourful figure in the pop world expressed this view: 'The man at the BBC responsible for pop presentation doesn't know the difference between a crotchet and a bull's arse.'

Unfortunately, there has been no comparable survey of composers' earnings since our study, but I am told that composition as a largely part-time occupation remains a dominant characteristic amongst PRS members.

PRS, BBC AND PRT

Having completed the earnings survey, the next task was to examine the 'market' for performance of music by the broadcasting system, which meant effectively the BBC, though independent

broadcasters were beginning to pay non-negligible sums to the
PRS by the early 1970s.

Faced with a bargaining situation with a powerful buyer, the
PRS clearly had to seek agreement with the BBC about the value
of performed music. First of all this required agreement about
the definition of output. In the reference made to the Performing
Right Tribunal in 1967, which was made necessary because
both parties could not agree, the PRS had argued that 'output'
consisted of the number of broadcasting hours weighted by an
audience factor. While the BBC agreed with this, a dispute arose
as to whether the audience factor weighting should be based on
'actual audience' (BBC argument) or 'potential audience' (PRS
argument). These alternative weightings reflected completely
different views of the meaning of 'output', despite their common
base. To the PRS, output was represented by sales of performance
to the BBC. If the BBC increased the number of hours of broadcast
music a derived demand would be set up for more performance
material so that output could be said to have increased. The BBC
measure, on the other hand, was based on its output *to its listeners*.
An increase in the hours of performance might or might not result
in a proportional increase in the size of audience. It therefore
preferred a weighting factor based on actual audiences.

The BBC's position seemed reasonable enough, until it is
realised, as I pointed out, that it had monopolistic control over
output. Its financial position was not dependent on the volume
of output, using its own measure, for it was financed, as it
still is, by a compulsory licence fee, which it negotiated, not
with its audience, but with the government. The BBC might
respond to pressures from composers to increase performance
hours and might be restricted in the use of recordings through
'needle time' restrictions negotiated separately with Phonograph
Performances Ltd, but its degree of control over the volume of
output was still formidable.

Determining ground rules for negotiating the pricing of output, whatever definition were finally agreed, presented an even
more difficult problem. In the post Second World War period, the
convention had been accepted that the royalty payable to the PRS
by the BBC should be a fixed charge per receiving licence over a
period of years. This charge was rather like a specific tax on the
individual, but not based on the value of the licence. The amount

of royalty received by composers depended on the growth in the volume of licence sales and therefore on the honesty of the listening public and the vigilance of a body, the Post Office, not under the normal economic pressures which would have maximised the sale of licences. At the same time, the composer did not obtain any advantage from adjustments in the licence fee itself, the adjustment of which was made more frequently and independently of any adjustment in the royalty payment.

The rate of inflation in the 1960s eroded the real value of the royalty payment by the BBC to the PRS so that when it came to seeking a compensating adjustment in 1967, an increase of nearly 50 per cent in the 'tax' per licence was sought, which the BBC understandably contested. The PRS was faced with the same psychological resistance encountered by local authorities when, in order to increase revenue from the old local rate, they were forced to alter the rate poundage, even in times when ratepayers' incomes were rising much faster than their rate burdens.

What I was able to do to help was to buttress the PRS's case for a royalty formula which removed the disadvantages of discontinuous ajustments. This was done by inventing an *'ad valorem'* formula by which royalty receipts were linked automatically to changes in the volume and the value of PRS music used by the BBC. I put forward a simple formula:

$$\text{PRS royalty} = \text{BBC revenue} \times \frac{A - B}{A} \times C$$

where
  A = broadcasting hours per period
  B = total non-music broadcasting hours per period
  C = royalty percentage

This formula turned out to be very similar to one which the PRS had put forward to the PRT shortly before I had appeared on the scene. Clearly there could be problems of definition when it came to items 'A' and 'B' but the major discussion would be over 'C'. It would however concentrate the minds of either side on what factors governed the value of music performed by the BBC. The PRS had always placed particular emphasis on the need to compensate composers for changes in the cost of living, but could hardly expect the BBC to pay up unless it could assume that the licence fee also reflected changes in the cost of living. I suggested

that the formula might also take into account the relative position
of composers in the scale of earnings, the onus of proof being on
the BBC to demonstrate why composers should experience a fall
in relative earnings through time! I was bound to emphasise that
any kind of job evaluation approach had a spurious accuracy
about it. The choice of job characteristics which would determine
whether or not an occupation had changed its economic status
in the income hierarchy is entirely arbitrary and is reflected in
the widespread disagreement over the weightings to apply to
each characteristic. In addition, the very concept of evaluation
suggests that subjective value judgments have to be made
and there is no scientific way of ranking such judgments. In
disabusing the PRS of the idea that an economist could offer
cogent reasons to support a job evaluation approach, at least I
was putting them on guard against pseudo-scientific arguments.
Therefore an argument about the composers' 'right' to have
the relative standard of living taken into account was based
on a subjective view of distributional equity though it might
inspire enquiry into the changes in the quality and quantity of
composers' output.

A body such as the PRT trying to resolve a dispute about the
'market price' of musical composition faces an impossible job
in trying to guess at what would represent the equivalent to a
'competitive' solution representing the outcome of transactions
between willing buyers and sellers. It will understandably take
the existing situation as the point of departure for any arbitration
and seek compromises which do not require either side to face
major changes in their economic position or at least to have to
make them quickly. Moreover, it must somewhere along the line
take public opinion into account, particularly when one side, the
BBC, had so much discretion in how it spent the public's money,
and the other, the PRS, was claiming a not inconsiderable cut of
the proceeds.

Nevertheless, the PRT, which had taken a firm line in favour
of the 'specific tax' approach in their 1967 decision about the
payment of royalties by the BBC, changed its tune to a remarkable
extent in 1972. Although my report was not submitted until May
of that year, the advantage of continuous contact with the client
was demonstrated by my being in a position to help with the
submission to the PRT which had to be made well before I was

due to report. In particular, the PRS, as well as advocating a formula which required the BBC to pay a proportion of its revenue for music, adjusted for 'music use', argued that the proportionate charge should reflect the relative earnings position of composers. The point was taken by the PRT and mentioned in its March 1972 decision. It commended the PRS formula as having 'the merit of simplicity' though it rejected a further 'music-use' weighting in arriving at the final payment. A straight unweighted formula, they argued, 'would be sufficient to cover not merely the rise in the cost and the standard of living, but also an increased use of PRS music by the BBC'.

The PRS did not publish our Report and, for confidentiality reasons, were unwilling to publish the details of our composers' survey. But they did sponsor the publication of *The Composer in the Market Place*, which Ron Weir and I carved out of part of the Report and our separate studies of the economic history of the composer; and Asa (now Lord) Briggs wrote a charming Preface to it. The book was launched in 1975 at a splendid lunch presided over by Sir Arthur Bliss and held in the Savoy, where, years before, I had been passed by Arnold Goodman as fit to begin my curious journey into the realm of professional music. Ron, not long launched on a lecturing career, and his young wife entered the River Room dazzled by the splendour of the surroundings and the well groomed staff ready to do our bidding. It recalled for him the description of a famous ballroom scene in Brussels. 'I expect', he said, 'that any moment a dragoon will rush in and announce that the Battle of Waterloo has commenced!' Perhaps this was some small compensation for his being mercilessly exploited by one of his professors.

Of course, a lot has happened in the intervening years, and I was only to be concerned with one part of the PRS's activities. Obviously, the growth in the number of broadcasting outlets and the addition to terrestrial broadcasting of new methods of transmission, cable and satellite, complicate the negotiations over broadcasting royalties and the process of monitoring broadcasts for the purpose of arriving at a fair distribution of royalties to individual composers and lyricists. One can imagine the difficulties of negotiation when one encounters the statement that exemption from the broadcasting rights is obtained for 'words written for the purpose of a commercial advertisement unless such words are sung to music specially written for a commercial advertisement or to non-copyright music and the sung performance has a duration of less than five seconds' (PRS, 1989, p. 41)! But two vestiges of the 1970s controversy remain which arose out of my consulting work. Firstly, negotiations of royalties are based on the size of the *potential* audience of the television or radio network. Secondly, such negotiations take account not only of the cost but also of the standard of living of composers, in the latter case with reference to the index of average earnings. I have to confess that both these propositions, while they would naturally occur to an economist used to statistical measurement, represent argument by persuasion and reflect, as I have emphasised, a purely subjective view of the equity of the composers' case. That is not to say that I believe that composers should be exempted from the requirement of providing music which is meant to be enjoyable and/or stimulating if the public is to pay for it. Nor should they be placed in the position where they can hold the public up to ransom. There is a long way to go before that could happen.

CODETTA: A CONUNDRUM

I have it on good authority that a well known composer, a Council Member of the PRS, and therefore a strong supporter of composers' rights, has a brother who makes furniture. 'Why,' he argues 'should you, my brother, be able to charge for the performance of your music while I cannot charge people for sitting down on my chairs after I have sold them?' It makes a good examination question! Perhaps this chapter will help furnish the reader with the composer's answer.

7

VALSE TRISTE
How to Lose Friends and Alienate People

AN UNFORCED CONFESSION

A strange document was found in George Street, Edinburgh, a few months back which seems to have fallen out of the briefcase of a careless psychoanalyst. Public duty compels me, like the *Daily Mirror*, to reveal its contents. The patient appears to have been in great distress:

'I was taught that it is easier to give than to receive – what a load of rubbish. If you want a passport to popularity don't have my job of doling out public money to arts organisations. It's rather like feeding hungry uncaged lions. The only thing you can do is to dish out the meat and then run for your life. The Bard says somewhere: 'rich gifts wax poor when givers prove unkind' – that's what 'they' think of you . . .

Take Glasgow-based clients. They're a funny lot. Some don't make moan at all and seem almost trusting, and others write you polished letters which you know mean the Glasgae equivalent of 'A'll smash yer face in'. Edinburgh is different; very sniffy letters with postscripts like 'I would have you know that my Chairman is the brother-in-law of the Secretary of State's cook' – menacing words presaging a sleepless night for me. Anonymous letters come from my home town, Dundee, not noted for doubles entendres – 'yer a' a load of peely-wally faced poofs'. Missed out Aberdeen, did I? Well, they never actually get round to turning slanders into libels by writing anything down. You'll have heard the story of the cello-player in the Royal Scottish Orchestra who dreamt he was moonlighting in Aberdeen in a local production of *The Messiah*. He woke up to find it was perfectly true!

Gaels – beware Gaels. You heap riches on them, even to the extent of financing an annual week-long ceilidh (bash) for Gaelic poets from the Isles and from Eire. You're liable to get a letter ending 'It is as well that Gaeldom knows who are her real enemies!' . . . Ma La Contessa Elisabetta di Dalchita (trs. Dalkeith?)! Now she's a real bonny fighter for her ballet company. That 'Belle Dame Sans Merci', that Terpischorean Turandot – better answer all her riddles to her satisfaction or you get yer heid chopped off! Nessun Dorma at the Arts Council when she is on the rampage. Answer her letters right away or you'll get FAXED – pages of the stuff arrive which we have to pay for. Question: can one sue anyone for faxual harrassment?

These ingrates have powerful allies. There are the ACRONYMANIACS – Advisory Council for the Arts in Scotland (ACAS), Council of Scottish Local Authorities (COSLA) – for all I know there may be a Borders Association for Ladies Literate in Scots (B _ _ _ _). Once got a letter and misread the heading which I thought was SALVE. How nice – a music group specializing in Renaissance church music perhaps – *Salve Regina* etc. etc. . . . NO NO a bruising letter from the Scottish Arts Lobby (SALVO) a terrifying tribe of taciturn toughs – Dear Sir: why have you not extracted £2b. minimum out of the pockets of an unsuspecting public in order to reduce (somewhat) the chronic state of underfunding in the arts. (Underfunded – the word should be banned – we're a' underfunded.) PS you are a Philistine. What did the poor Philistines do to deserve this reputation – all Schumann's fault wasn't it – ask one of the music critics if there is still one interested in anything other than jazz . . . .

Then there are CRITICS. An arts journalist is someone who writes unintelligibly about the inexplicable. The visual arts critics are the worst – you want the latest arts buzzword, they'll have it: 'the crypto-modernist fetishism manifested in X's latest biodegradable sculpture object is a deliberate digression from X's principal obsession with societal side issues such as voyeurism amongst neo-vorticists' . . . Gott in Himmel! They see conspiracies everywhere. One arty-farty fellow wrote a piece about this cloven-footed quangoman actually claiming that I deliberately chose my hobby list in *Who's Who* in order to con the world into believing that I was a caring person. It's not the blackening of reputation that worries me but his sheer incompetence in trying to prove it. Look at the list: 'trying to write music' – the man must be a public menace; 'wine spotting' – the man's just a drunk; 'hill-walking' – the environment is in danger. Looks as if far from caring, I should be in care. (Was it Osbert Sitwell who said about critics: 'oblivion is waiting for you' – ha ha!)

I've not finished. There are still POLITICIANS! The House of Commons is well named - what a common lot they generally are! They write to you at the drop of a hat (or, rather, vote).

'Dear Sir

It has been drawn to my attention that the great international event in the form of the Tannochbrae Thespians Post-Brechtian interpretation of *Getting Gertie's Garter* is not to receive your support. I am astonished at this inept decision and will obviously have to press for a public enquiry . . . drone, drone . . . .

Yours sincerely (what?)

Hamish Mc—

PS Lloyd George knew my mother.

Do you remember, vaguely, a politician called Ron Brown? Exemplary MP, never wrote once to us. Vastly entertaining, too, and should have been offered a grant by us to support his contribution to serious, original dramatics. Nationalist politicians, understandably, are breathing down my neck the whole time. They at least have a clear idea what they want. I have seen a secret document signed 'Paulus Scotus' which states that as soon as the Scots Ministry of Culture is set up, *Coronation Street* is to be blacked out on all TV screens. In its place 750-episode version of *The Thrie Estaitis* will be supplied, with Sean Connery playing all the main parts, except Chastity. Difficult casting problem here – how about La Contessa?

Yes, yes, you want to know what my problem is. Don't I feel better getting that all off my chest? Yes, but that's not why I'm seeking help. Why am I here? My trouble is that when you meet all these people – artists, musicians, even critics, politicians and lobbyists – HOW NICE AND CHARMING MOST OF THEM CAN BE!

A GLUTTON FOR PUNISHMENT

I have never consulted a psychoanalyst or psychiatrist though I have had the curious experience of being asked by three psychiatrists to help them sort out their personal problems. Which category of personality this places me in, I would not like to consider and it is hardly of relevance here. The making of the 'unforced confession' above never really took place, but it does summarise some of my short-tempered over-reactions to the next phase of my encounters with the world of culture, including music. Why, I need to ask myself, did I ever choose to become a member of a quango like the Arts Council of Great Britain and simultaneously Chairman of the Scottish Arts Council? I need to offer an answer to this question if only to explain how my attitude to public funding of the arts had developed and, subsequently, how little I was able to achieve. First, let me say something about the background to the appointment. The Arts Council of Great Britain (ACGB) was founded in August 1946 and grew out of the wartime body, the Council for the

Encouragement of Music and the Arts (CEMA), which was largely
the brainchild of the famous economist, John Maynard Keynes.
Indeed, up to the time of his death in March 1946, he combined
the frightening and exhausting task of negotiating suitable terms
for the famous post-war loans from the USA designed to offset
the economic damage of the Second World War, with the almost
daily provision of advice on how to set up what became the ACGB
(see Mary Glasgow, 1975). While Keynes as an economist is
largely associated with his insistence on the short-run economic
position for, in his famous words, 'in the long run we are
dead', towards the end of his life he seemed to have become
preoccupied with the long-run problem of how, given growing
prosperity, the fruits of that prosperity could be manifested in a
vast improvement in the quality of life for all. There is a ring of
an uneasy conscience about his words, as if he perceived that the
joys of civilised living had come too easily to him. The problem
was how to bring a prosperous-growing public to see that they
too, could, if they wanted to, share his good fortune. What
fascinates me about Keynes's position is the emphasis placed
on devising forms of public support which would 'prime the
pump of private spending'. The initial problem was for the state
to indulge in a widespread capital programme which would
ensure that artistic performances could be given in properly
constructed concert halls, opera houses and theatres. Subsidies
to single companies were only temporary devices, rather like
research and development expenditure, to give them a start in
life. Permanent subsidies to single companies concentrated in
the metropolis were to be avoided. The purpose of state support
for the arts was to inform the public how they could spend their
money wisely and well for their own benefit, and subsidies could
then wither away. Keynes looked forward to the day when only a
small amount of administrative expenditure by government on
cultural propaganda was necessary. Keynes's view is obviously
a counsel of perfection but it offers a goal, a star to follow, which,
if never reached, is worth the attempt. My agreement with this
view has always been whole-hearted.

Keynes's view on the role of the body which he largely created
was never adopted by the ACGB. It has always perceived its role
as being the perpetual funder of arts institutions which would
never by themselves be able to raise all their funds from the

box-office and private sponsorship. Furthermore, by and large it has considered that the best way of doing this, compatible with its terms of reference to 'develop and improve the knowledge and understanding of the arts and to increase the accessibility of the arts to the public throughout Britain', is to offer grants directly to such institutions.

Without entering into a detailed examination of the anthropology of state quangos, it is not difficult to understand why. Granted that a start has to be made by offering direct grants to all manner of theatre companies, orchestras and the like, a vested interest develops in a particular way of doing things. There is an immense attraction, from which few people are immune, in having power to guide the destiny of others, and to be able to offer the laudatory reason that in so doing our cultural tradition is being preserved and extended, all of which salves the conscience of any worries about becoming a patrician. This may be a convenient rationalization, but one might be more impressed with an honest claim by members of the ACGB with professional experience who claim to 'know better' than the public what is good for them, that they alone can distinguish between good and bad art, and must resist attempts by politicians to limit artistic freedom. They would be deprived of the role of guardians of our culture if the predominant form of public support consisted of grants to consumers to spend on a given range of cultural activities or of tax relief to individuals and firms who would have freedom to support those artistic endeavours which appealed to them. Likewise, the officials who advise ACGB would be left to become mere issuers of certificates to 'recognised' institutions eligible to attract consumer spending supported by either grants or tax relief.

My views on such matters were not unknown so that I was much surprised when I was asked to become Chairman of the Scottish Arts Council and, in consequence, a member of the Arts Council of Great Britain. As reported, I had been a member of the SAC for a short while before my civil service appointment in 1973 obliged me to resign, and had some reputation for being knowledgeable about the economic problems of the arts as perhaps the previous chapters indicate, but I was hardly a favourite son. I am told that in 1976 when I returned from Whitehall to academic life, there was a suggestion that I should become a member of the ACGB, but the then Secretary of State for Education, Shirley Williams, whose Ministry was then responsible for arts expenditure, blocked the appointment. That was not entirely surprising as my Whitehall appointment covered the giving of economic advice to Mrs Williams as Secretary of State for Consumer Affairs, and she may not have forgiven me for refusing to criticise the official calculations of the cost-of-living index and to offer alternative calculations likely to be more congenial to the Cabinet. An attempt to reinstate me as a member of the SAC was also blocked, ostensibly on the grounds that I would be returning to live in York which was outwith the borders of God's country. That had not mattered in 1972, but devolution of government to Scotland was not such a sensitive political issue then. There is no doubt that by 1986 my ideas were more congenial to the government in power, though, as a member of no party, my name was not simply being extracted from the Whips' List. While the appointment was treated with some caution by the cultural cognoscenti north of the Border – entirely understandable – it was not likely to be enthusiastically received further south. The ex-Secretary General of the ACGB, Sir Roy Shaw, to whom I had delivered the report on inflation mentioned in Chapter 5, collared me at some Arts Council 'bash' and remarked pointedly that he never thought he would live to see the day when I was appointed a member of the ACGB.

I saw the post as an opportunity to try to interest the ACGB and the SAC in considering more seriously a policy designed eventually to do us out of business, by concentrating much more of our resources on subsidy methods which would 'alter the preference functions', as economists would put it, of the public so that there was a good chance that the arts could become largely self-supporting. As Samuel Johnson said about re-marriage, this was a clear case of 'the triumph of hope over experience'. While that was the principal reason for my interest, I cannot deny that I looked forward to extending my own experience and enjoyment of the arts, one of the obvious requirements as well as a 'perk' of such a post, and to examine at closer quarters another part of the machinery of government which was bound to engage my professional interest. Whatever one may think about bureaucracy in the abstract I must stress that a large proportion of officials concerned with the arts are deeply devoted to spending public money effectively and efficiently according to the rules laid down for them, while being placed in a position where they get precious little thanks from those who benefit. Whatever my ideological commitment to change, the immediate task as Chairman of the SAC was to see that the Council commanded their loyalty and respect whilst making it clear that the Council in the end had to decide how to interpret its terms of reference.

At this stage it would be natural to retail my experiences in trying to carry out the Chairman's duties, in the course of which there would be a wonderful opportunity to offer pen pictures of the 'greatish and goodish' who revel in the role of being fairy godparents to the arts. However, I shall stick to my theme of 'paying the piper' and explain how I completely failed to convince anyone that we should follow the prescriptions – for the funding of the arts at least – of John Maynard Keynes. My comments on personalities are incidental to the theme of this chapter, and this will give a false impression of my relations with members of both Councils and officials which in all important respects were cordial.

I should mention that on one matter I have to take issue with Keynes. A longstanding problem in arts funding has been the insistence of the Scots that they should have a prescribed 'cut' of the entire budget of the ACGB before any allocations are made and that SAC should be left to allocate the cut as they think fit. Towards the end of my term of office (1986–92) I put it to Richard Luce, the then Minister of Arts and Libraries, that the ACGB should be federalised and that the three Councils – the ACGB, the SAC and the Welsh Arts Council – should receive their budget directly from his Department. This accorded with my political views as a devolutionist. This issue was a source of annoyance to Keynes, as it has been to a whole succession of ACGB Council members and administrators. As Mary Glasgow records, Keynes got very fed up with the insistent demands of the Scots for what he regarded as privileged treatment. Here are some quotations from the letters she received from him: 'So long as they do not require the Chairman to wear a kilt at one meeting out of ten, it is, I think, a matter of words', but Keynes added, 'I always find the question of Scotland . . . too tiresome to concentrate on easily. I would rather hand them over their share of money, leaving them to stew in their own feeble juice than agree to a separatist precedent which would allow them to get the best of both worlds'. It is a pity that he did not live long enough for him to eat his words about the 'feeble juice', and, characteristically, I am sure he would have done so had he witnessed the flourishing of the arts in post Second World War Scotland.

'CONSUMER SOVEREIGNTY': AN IMPOSSIBLE IDEAL?

I have at various points in my narrative expressed the value judgment that any approximation to the kind of cultural nirvana which artists and their admirers wish to see can never be achieved, without sacrificing the virtues of democracy, unless the enthusiastic and continuous support of a knowledgeable public is ensured. At the same time, if that support were to grow stronger, the need for state subsidy would diminish, if not entirely disappear. This judgment not only pervades my views on culture, and on music in particular, but extends to all personal services, such as health and education, provided by government. For me a liberal society is one in which individuals choose for themselves and are responsible for their choices. That does not preclude state intervention to redress gross inequalities in wealth and income but the emphasis of such intervention should be on helping individuals to help themselves. It means a long-term programme of moving away from state production of services towards state support, where necessary, to help individuals to plan their own lives. For example, I developed, with my close friend Jack Wiseman, one of the first schemes for education vouchers which would combine full access to educational resources by the very poorest with a large measure of freedom of choice in schooling. These ideas were new and met hostile criticism in the 1960s, but are common currency across the whole political spectrum today, particularly after the fall of Communism. The one area where these are spectacularly absent is in the field of culture. I had an opportunity to develop these ideas concurrently with my appointment to the the ACGB and the SAC. They obtained some notoriety in the Report of the Committee on Financing the BBC (Home Office, 1986), which I chaired, and in which the Committee supported in general a move towards a consumer-driven broadcasting system. The reaction by the broadcasting pundits gave a foretaste of the problems one would face in extending the concept of consumer choice to the performing and creative arts. I wrote a number of papers for different sorts of audience re-reviewing some of the ideas which appear in the earlier chapters of this book, and circulated these to long-suffering officials, to some members of the Councils, and to the Minister of Arts and Libraries. One had to be aware that, even if the principle of consumer sovereignty might be received favourably, politicians and officials would be concerned with practicalities. Many economists having presented the principles of the logic of choice would maintain that it is not their business to be involved with policy implementation. I believe this to be a convenient rationalisation, though I recognise that the comparative advantage of most economists may lie in logical exercises rather than in administrative innovations. They do rather remind me of the splendid story told by Martin Shubik, the Princeton economist:

> The owl was the wisest of animals. A centipede with 99 sore feet came to him seeking advice. 'Walk for two weeks one inch above the ground; the air under your feet and the lack of pressure will cure you,' said the owl. 'How am I to do that?' asked the centipede. 'I have solved your conceptual problem, do not bother me with trivia concerning implementation,' replied the owl. (Shubik, 1985, p. 615).

I am well aware that the principle of consumer sovereignty as presented in economic treatises usually considers only the case where tastes and preferences of consumers are given. Clearly this is a very restrictive assumption as we all know that in the course of gaining experience in spending income, not only may we learn how to improve the efficiency of choice, but our tastes develop and change. The formation of choice, however, depends not only on learning by doing but also on the investment made in our education. There could be a considerable consensus for the view that to the extent that education provides benefits over and above those bestowed on the educated, there is as good a case for using some educational resources for cultural alongside other kinds of education. Tibor Scitovsky who, as I observed earlier, made gentle fun at my expense, is noted for his thesis that the human propensity for excitement and danger, while often the cause of violent behaviour which society generally abhors, could be satisfied by providing artistic outlets. The education system should have the task of teaching 'new consumption skills' which channel the drive for excitement into participation in and appreciation of the arts. He certainly had something more in mind than what is now a common form of therapy in our better prisons though he does not elaborate on details (see Scitovsky, 1983).

That is at least one argument by a much-respected economist which commands wide support. I have met few strict libertarians who would argue that there must be no element of compulsion in the teaching of their children, and, even if they regard formation of taste as a family responsibility, they generally are sympathetic to education in the arts. By itself this does not support an argument that the collective interest requires state subsidies for this purpose, any more than for education as a whole, but, however educational services are provided, it suggests a close link between professional arts companies, including of course those providing music of all kinds, and educational establishments. I was particularly keen on assuming office to find out how such links could be forged. One could describe all sorts of exciting ventures in arts education for younger people which, it is hoped, will exploit their talents and interests so that they will form an appreciative though critical audience of what is offered to them by artistic innovators of all kinds. I concentrate attention on one scheme which was already in being when I became Chairman of the SAC and which seemed to me to be fully in line with my own philosophy. In the early eighties the Scottish Community Educational Council, through a magazine for 'Young Scots', publicised arts events that were considered of particular interest to young people. The SAC devised a companion scheme by which, for the price of £5 a year, young people could obtain a Young Scots Card which would be recognised by co-operating arts centres, arts companies and the like, as a method for obtaining discounts on admission prices. It was therefore a kind of voucher, but the cost to the taxpayer, as represented by publicising the scheme and negotiating with cultural bodies, was minimal. For arts companies, unless playing every night to full houses, price discrimination designed to attract additional custom increases their marginal revenue without adding to their marginal costs and could, in the longer run, help them in audience-building. To the young people, they could choose freely a pattern of artistic enjoyment according to their own tastes and preferences. There was likely to be little opposition from those who had to pay the higher prices for the same seats as the young, and I suspect that many of us derive satisfaction from a form of cross-subsidization which encourages the development of their artistic interests.

Later on the scheme was complemented by a 'windfall' donation to the SAC from the estate of an American lady married to a Scot. This is administered separately as the Shepley-Shepley Trust – the name of the donor – and it was decided to devote all its income initially to the support of artistic ventures put forward by young people between the ages of sixteen and twenty-five. These youth arts projects were not circumscribed by the cultural ambience of the SAC and have extended to pop art and music of a kind which might engender an interest in more testing areas of artistic perception. More important still, the committee judging whether or not any youth venture was worth support has a majority of young people, and one could not fail to be impressed by the quality of their decisions which required them to be particularly tough on their own kind, given the remarkable response to the scheme.

The arts component of the Young Scot scheme was the brainchild of Tim Mason, then Director of the SAC, backed by my predecessor, Gerald Elliot, and had strong support from the SAC itself, matched by their enthusiasm for the use of Shepley-Shepley money in a way which young people themselves thought sensible, as Tim and I had proposed. It was schemes of this kind already in being which emboldened me to try to push further towards allocating a much greater proportion of our funds to support of the public, leaving them free to spend them on an agreed 'slate' of artistic activities.

I had several interesting discussions with Tim about supporting consumers rather than producers. His political philosophy and – on this he would put great weight – his experience of arts administration made him very sceptical but, rare for persons working under great pressure and responsibilities, he liked a good argument even if it questioned his own way of doing things.

Suggestions for consumer support have usually centred on voucher systems which entitle individuals to 'spend' them on services of their choice from a 'shopping list' (see Peacock, 1969, West, 1985). In the case of the arts, vouchers would entitle consumers to a reduction in the price of 'cultural goods' from a prescribed list provided by the Arts Councils. The arts organisation providing the cultural service – drama, music, cinema – would exchange the vouchers for cash from the grant-giving arts bodies. (There are other possibilities, such as some form of tax relief on consumer arts expenditure, but I shall not discuss these.) Of course, there is a patrician element still left in the system, in the choice of arts activities eligible for voucher support. However, it is arguable that consumers/taxpayers may prefer professionals to certify which forms of cultural activity are worth supporting, in the same way as they would for many forms of consumer goods, e.g. cars and computers, where their utility is increased by information and advice about choices. This can never be a complete argument unless one can show that such information and advice would not be obtainable in suitable form from private sources. But rather than debate the point, let it be granted that there is public support for some such certifying body. This would not preclude, as I have suggested several times in this book, built-in protection against any monopoly of cultural ideas, for this could be obtained by frequent changes in membership of the body concerned and the encouragement of open debate on the scope, form and content of the certification process. There *should be* a ferment of discussion on aesthetic and cultural matters for choices in the end rest on subjective judgments as much as on professional knowledge. What is more, to the extent that these ideas can be translated into new artistic ventures, the process of certification should not discriminate in favour of established companies at the expense of 'interlopers' who challenge what is presently on offer to the public.

To return to the nitty-gritty of consumer subsidies. To whom and how does one distribute vouchers? As the argument has been developed, it is implied that every adult citizen has a property right in vouchers which entails some system of national distribution. This could be expensive, unless the minimum economic cost paid by consumers is to take the trouble to apply for them, perhaps at local offices or agents of the subsidising authority.

The second problem is whether or not vouchers should be tradeable between consumers. This is not an issue in the case, say, of education vouchers for schools, because educational consumption is compulsory, whereas it is inconceivable that adults should be forced to attend artistic events. Preventing transferability of vouchers would require unacceptable bureaucratic interference and expense. Transferability, however, would encourage the setting up of a market in vouchers through which those with relatively strong preferences for cultural goods – at present largely the well-educated and well-heeled – would receive a windfall benefit, provided, as seems likely, they could purchase vouchers at below their face value. (There is an additional incentive to enter this market for vouchers would be an untaxed source of income!) It could be, I suppose, that those with comparatively less knowledge of artistic events may have their interest aroused in the events themselves if there is the alternative opportunity of selling their vouchers, but the main objective of a voucher scheme would be frustrated if the market became an active one. A final general problem concerns the relation between the amount of the voucher and the costs of attending artistic events by the receiver. Artistic events tend to be concentrated in populous areas where covering their costs is made much easier by the volume of business. This means that those outwith such areas have to bear the cost of time and travel in order to attend them. The value of the voucher therefore differs according to the individuals' valuation of these extra costs but trying to equalise the value would produce a system of great complexity especially if it had to take account of subjective valuations of such costs.

I had to admit that these were real problems and not simply a check-list of standard objections devised by obstructive bureaucrats – not that I regarded Tim and his colleagues in such a light. He was sympathetic to the use of a voucher system or its near equivalent if targeted at particular groups who could be clearly identified. Indeed, it is common practice for subsidising bodies, including local authorities, to try to equalise access to artistic events through the use of transport subsidies to local arts clubs or music societies. Music, it turns out, is a good example of successful targeting. Music ensembles other than large symphony orchestras and opera companies can travel to audiences, but there is no reason why music societies should not be awarded a general grant which would allow them to make their own choices of ensemble and programme. Nor is there any reason why private artistic foundations interested in extending knowledge of the arts should not direct more of their activities to audience creation combined with audience choice along similar lines.

However, it was soon clear to me that all these difficulties, which would exist if one were designing a system of consumer support *de novo*, pale into insignificance alongside the change that this would make in existing practice with all the attendant problems of coping with vested interests. In examining the various interests, let me make it clear that nothing that I say about them leads me to doubt the integrity of those who support them, though I would like them to act otherwise.

Members of Council

For both the ACGB and the SAC, the major proportion of members are appointed because of their expertise in and/or strong commitment to a particular art-form. Understandably they fight for funding for that particular art-form and see themselves as balancing the interests of both producers and consumers of culture. Consumer subsidies are simply not compatible with their objectives. Such subsidies diffuse support for a particular art-form by allowing a range of freedom of choice amongst different art-forms and so restrict Council members' influence. They also remove the guarantee that any particular cultural producer will receive state funding.

Administrators

A fair proportion of them are recruited from the ranks of creative and performing artists. Their long-term career prospects seem likely to embrace the prospect of returning to cultural production. If they were to become enthusiasts for reducing subsidies to arts organisations they would hardly endear themselves to their peer group or to prospective employers. In this respect, the case of the Northern Arts Association's 'coupon' scheme, by which young persons could present coupons at theatre box-offices which gave them a reduction in price, is instructive. The theatres involved were highly supportive, for the scheme created a new audience as well as extra income from the redemption of the coupons. The reason for discontinuance in 1980 is revealing. It meant a diversion of funds away from support for individual artists. As Eddie West (1985) suggests, it is difficult not to draw the conclusion that the decision was taken because diversion to young consumers reduced administrative discretion and therefore the power given to bureaucrats to favour producers.

Politicians

They would naturally respond to pressure from producer interests if reallocation of subsidies to consumers meant that arts organisations in their area were to lose custom and begin job-shedding. Cohesive interest groups such as arts unions are likely to be much more vocal than consumers who are notoriously difficult to organise. But the matter goes deeper than that. In my experience, politicians, who understandably wish to regard themselves as cultured persons, are normally deeply sensitive to allegations of 'philistinism', and join subsidised companies in the hue and cry against 'insensitive' arts administrators when the latter, usually for cogent reasons, have to question whether a particular company is giving the taxpayer value for money.

Of course the sceptics were right and I made little headway, but the reasons do not lie solely in the perceived difficulties of turning a contestable principle into practice. On the SAC we did manage occasionally to set aside a crowded agenda of urgent matters to discuss questions of principle but the discussion tended to be geared towards how to maintain consistency in the application of existing policies, given our terms of reference. That was a difficult enough issue, without opening up the whole question, as I was implying, as to whether those terms of reference were wholly sensible. I learnt much from these discussions. So far as our parent body, the ACGB, which suffered even more from the immediate pressures caused by clamorous and influential clients, mainly national companies, was concerned, such opportunities were rare indeed. When they did occur, on occasional 'retreats' to aesthetically pleasing locations, either some immediate crisis dominated discussion or we became bogged down in particularities. In my nearly six years of office, I can only recall one paper being submitted on broad matters of policy by a Council member – myself. It did eventually produce a tangible result in the form of the first national survey of public attitudes to the arts; but I never got anywhere with the idea that public perception of the arts should be translated into consumer power to choose which art-form to support.

THE SUBSIDY 'GAME'

A move towards consumer funding seeming to be a distant prospect, I had to concentrate attention, along with other members of the SAC and the ACGB, on supporting officials in running an efficient system of direct subsidies to a widely heterogenous list of individuals and companies in the arts sector. This could range from a single artist who could obtain a grant to develop some genre of painting to a major symphony orchestra of 100 players, with a vast repertoire and a long tradition. Of course, for the large bulk of clients of arts councils, income derived from selling pictures or seats at the box-office is still of major importance. Latterly, too, the UK government has been interested in state lotteries as a method of funding at least part of the arts budget. Nevertheless, to the extent that Arts Councils monies figure largely in the current account of funded bodies, the direct subsidy continues to predominate.

There is an immediate dilemma presented by the attitude of funding bodies and those that they fund, which is simply the modern equivalent of the tension between patron and artist which must be as old as art itself. The funding body has a limited budget alongside the funding requests from organisations and individuals who would pass the acid test of being, by judgment of peers, worth funding. It must not only choose between different art-forms and between alternative potential recipients of support. As government money is involved, it is expected to demonstrate that the money is well spent, alongside the alternative uses of the money, i.e. support of other government services and/or lower taxation. The form of the 'rule' to be applied is that of the maximum 'output' – we have already explained the difficulties of this concept – consistent with the budget available. Giving content to that rule is another matter altogether.

If the optimum position of funding bodies is to make every penny count, that of the artist is to be placed in the comfortable position of being left alone to get on with the important job of maximising reputation with one's peers. There are echoes here of Stravinsky and Pound (see Chapter 2) claiming that the artist should be in no way accountable to those who support him. I am sure that many of us sympathise with creative and performing artists who feel that their talents are constrained by having to account for their material support. Nor, if opportunity allowed, would they necessarily seek to emulate Richard Wagner in his demands for munificent treatment from his patrons. Occasionally one hears of private patrons who are generous to a fault with artists and risk the possibility that they may be taken for a ride. They are, after all, free to use their resources as they please. The problem facing artists is that the analogy between private and state patronage does not hold, for Arts Councils are funded out of other people's money obtained by compulsory exaction. They also appear to share an intense dislike of being placed in the position that if they receive funding, some other artistic venture has to go without. Therefore, the decisions of the Arts Councils are constantly under fire, as they must inevitably be 'wrong' if deserving fellow-artists have to do without. In this case the messenger can never bring anything but bad news, or at least the bad news is more dramatic than the good.

Despite the 'owl story' which makes fun of prescriptions to improve the world which are devoid of content, I think that there is a lot to be said for trying to offer some kind of conceptual framework in order to explain the difficulties of developing some sensible way of using public money to support specific arts projects. It might look something like this:

(a) In broad terms a subsidy to a particular company, say an opera company, is presumably designed to influence the company to develop its artistic pursuits in accordance with the policy objectives of the funding body. In other words, the company – and this is important – is being asked to undertake certain functions that it would *not otherwise perform* – known in the trade as the principle of additionality. It would be a waste of resources, which have alternative uses, if the company would simply continue to do what it would have done without subsidy support.

(b) It logically follows that it must be possible to draw up a contract between 'the principal' (the subsidy authority) and 'the agent' (the arts company) by which the services rendered for the amount of subsidy received can be specified in terms

agreed by both parties. In the case of a direct subsidy based
on the principle of additionality, this carries the implication
that there is some quantitative connection between the extra
'output' to be delivered and the subsidy received.

(c) For the subsidy to be calculable in advance of delivery of
the 'output', then costs of producing the extra 'output' must
be known with reasonable certainty.

(d) For the subsidy to be 'efficient', then the principal must
be satisfied that the estimates of cost are the minimum
necessary to supply the extra 'output'.

(e) If the contract is to be renewed periodically, then the
principal will expect evidence to be provided by the agent
that the conditions of a past contract have been met, or if
they have not, that acceptable explanations can be given as
to why that is not the case.

You have seen it coming! Sticking to the logical order of things
makes for an uneasy relationship between principal and agent
with several potential sources of disagreement and therefore the
prospect of turbulent and protracted negotiation. Although, as
Chairman, I tended to be used as a Court of Appeal (but not
the final one!) or as the ultimate deterrent, whichever way one
looked at it, I was not normally involved in negotiation. I recall
one occasion on which I thought that the banging on the table
was going to be the prelude to fisticuffs.

The reasons for expecting confrontation are obvious enough
but worth exploring a little further. As the economist would
put it, the principal cannot expect otherwise unless two important conditions are fulfilled: (a) the agent's activities must
be perfectly observable so that any departure from the contract
can be detected; and (b) the production costs and the demand
conditions can be determined with perfect certainty. The first
condition offers the prospect of a 'moral hazard' problem well
known in insurance contracts. If the agent is the sole source
of information on costs, what incentive is there to reveal the
true minimum costs of production and, correspondingly, what
incentives exist for the principal to spend time and resources
in probing the quality of the estimates? The second condition
is also a strict one. The agent may be uncertain both about
the future costs of production and about demand conditions. It

follows that, apart from giving itself the benefit of the doubt in revealing its prospective costs and demand, the agent will have a strong incentive, given uncertain conditions, to seek protection from 'exogenous shocks', the incidence and timing of which may be unknown. In the case of negotiating a subsidy, the agent is likely to wish not only to build an allowance for risks in to cost estimates but to seek some kind of risk-sharing arrangement with the principal.

In my experience, the problems of moral hazard and uncertainty are particularly prevalent in the direct subsidisation of arts organisations and the incentives to solve these problems are blunted because of the understandable sensitivity of committees and officials to criticism – much of it disguised special pleading – from the worlds of culture if they have to take tough decisions. The example I give is based on fact, though it would be invidious for me to reveal the identity of those concerned or when and where the transactions took place! You will have to take it on trust that it is not atypical.

A funding body negotiates with, say, an orchestra about its annual grant. It begins by identifying the policy objectives which will be implemented through subsidising the company such as a guarantee of good standards of production, a 'reasonable' number of performances and audience 'spread'. It also builds in the constraints that the company must find 50 per cent of its revenue from other sources – box-office and private sponsorship. It asks for a budget based on these parameters, which must be available six months before the date of operation of the annual grant, if made, and that costings are broken down according to each programme, taking account of the expected number of performances. (These are just the broad details off any such request.)

The company might decide at the outset to adopt a 'high-risk' strategy and, while agreeing to provide budget estimates, may dispute the rationale of the funding body's approach on the grounds that the detail is unnecessary and the process of negotiation too protracted. (This is certainly a common opening gambit in negotiation!) This strategy would not be adopted if it were not known to work sometimes. The conditions for success seem to depend on the public standing of the company. It may engender public support by announcing some spectacular plans for the public's delectation without reference to cost and then rely on political pressure on the funding body to treat it generously. In short, it adopts a strategy of inviting other players to enter the bargaining game, but on their side. It may induce influential persons to support them by the offer of honorific posts in the organisation, such as 'patrons' or 'honorary presidencies'. However, let us proceed on the assumption that this strategy will have at most limited success and that the funding body is prepared to risk the obloquy of being tough and fair, bearing in mind that it has to estimate the opportunity cost measured in terms of the other companies which would be denied funding if the orchestra were 'generously' treated.

If the orchestra is to provide its budget on time, often doing so under protest, it must be conceded that it has to undertake a difficult exercise, for its accountants are much more likely to know how to keep books than to prepare budgets in a form which accords with economists' ideas of cost calculations. The committee of the funding body considering the estimates, who have several other exercises of this kind to consider, have now to seek advice on how reasonable the estimates are and whether the trade-offs between quality of production, number of productions and audience spread are in accordance with their own thinking. There is a presumption that the cost estimates err on the side of generosity to the company, justified on grounds of risk, and that revenue estimates are optimistic. (I have known companies simply to balance their budget by regarding earned income through box-office and sponsorship as a residual item!) Additionally, the company makes a pre-emptive strike on the evaluation of trade-offs, claiming that quality of production takes precedence over numbers of performances and audience spread – spread may involve travel to isolated venues with poor facilities.

Ideally, the reaction of the funding body should be to conduct a careful check on cost and revenue estimates, but the problem here is to know how this can be done without involving a massive amount of time and without inducing the orchestra to claim that a cost inquisition is an attack on the precious principle of artistic freedom. The lack of alternative potential bidders means that advisory staff have to rely on past experience with the orchestra or with similar companies, but the relevance of such experience may be limited. Basing the defence of a cost inquisition on the opportunity cost principle, including the proper use of taxpayers' money seems inadequate against the emotional arguments that deliberate interference with artistic decisions is the result.

Short of refusing to offer subsidy altogether, which is all but impossible with incumbents of long standing and professional repute, the strategy of the funding body has to rely on the argument that an 'inflated' budget to the orchestra means that other companies have to do without. This may make the company think twice about 'going public' by announcing their difficulties with the funding body though it may not make them any the less intransigent in negotiation. The associated tactics of the funding body are to demand from the company a statement as to how their plans would be revised if the subsidy on offer were some given percentage(s) above or below the requested amount. (It may excite their imagination overmuch if percentages *above* the request are brought into play!) Such a tactic may reveal at least some relevant information about the perceived costs of the company and how far they have taken the policy objectives seriously.

As with bargaining situations generally, it is difficult to forecast the exact outcome. The sticking point of the funding body will obviously depend on the pressure of other perceived funding obligations and the budget constraint. That of the orchestra will be some face-saving threshold, based on comparability with the awards made to other funded organisations, usually implying that the company receives at least something approaching the percentage increase in grant awarded to the funding body in aggregate, or at least the receipt of an amount which is indexed for inflation in their costs, if the funding body does not receive a real increase in its annual grant.

The obligations of the funding body clearly extend beyond scrutiny of the budget and the award of a conditional subsidy to the monitoring of the performance of the orchestra, alongside other subsidised companies. Ideally, the funding body wishes to obtain information not only to ascertain whether or not the 'contract' has been adhered to, but also as a way of improving appraisal procedures for use in later negotiations. This may be a partial substitute for not being able to fully check on the quality of information or to ascertain the reasonableness of the allowance for uncertainty built into the estimates. This presupposes that accurate accounting information is forthcoming quickly and in a form which facilitates comparison with budgeted estimates. In my experience it is a counsel of perfection to expect that the form, accuracy, speed of provision and content of accounting information will measure up to appraisal requirements. To the extent that it does, there will be further argument about its interpretation, given the problems encountered in specifying in the contract the exact relation between agreed objectives and the expected financial outcome.

It would be wrong to give the impression that the best to be expected in subsidy negotiation is a series of armed truces reluctantly agreed between the funders and the funded. Negotiation may entail a strong element of posturing on both sides, but it can also engender mutual trust and respect as one side realises the constraints which bind the other. Cordial relationships are possible and desirable, but they must not become cosy. Direct subsidies confer particular advantages on incumbent companies in receipt of state funding for decades but the fact of life remains that their performance must always be being compared with new ventures which offer a challenge to established ways of doing things and naturally expect to be given the opportunity of proving themselves.

A BRUSH WITH THE CULTURAL ESTABLISHMENT

One thing that really upset me in my experience with arts funding was the way in which so-called national companies would seek to alter the rules of the game by attempts to induce the government to force the Arts Councils to give them the top slice of the subsidy cake. The arguments that they used (and still use) remind me of the story of the Regius Professor of Surgery at an ancient university who produced a memorandum for a Royal Commission on the Remuneration of Doctors and Dentists containing a number of strong assertions about the relation between recruitment of doctors and their pay. He was asked repeatedly for tangible evidence and finally simply said: 'what evidence do you require, other than the fact that I have said so?' But the voice of authority and prestige does not always embody the ring of truth. The particular case with which I was involved was Covent Garden which may be interesting in itself, but also graphically illustrates the way in which the cultural establishment tries to rationalise the diversion of government support towards the art-forms from which they derive enjoyment and also personal prestige. After a particularly flagrant attempt at bullying the ACGB by Covent Garden, I wrote the following article at the request of *The Times*. It appeared on 14th March 1987:

Pruning the Garden

Much as I love the opera, I can produce only a slim case for special treatment of Covent Garden. I fully support the Arts Council policy of making the creative and performed arts more accessible and believe that its attempt at audience-building is incompatible with maintaining opera, the most expensive art-form, in the traditional way.

The new policy means more new ventures widely scattered geographically or mobile enough to reach isolated areas. It means building on the interests and aptitude of new audiences, particularly the young and relatively poor, whose taste for and experience of opera barely exists. Above all, when arts funding does not keep pace with inflation, it implies a cut in real resources for Covent Garden unless it can adapt to the new policy. The Garden must find it difficult to accept a change which reduces its expectations of a priority claim on resources and questions its artistic policies. By requesting funding increases well in excess of the percentage increase available to the Arts Council, it implicitly assumes that the new policy will have to be abandoned. The Garden, in common with other national companies, would be wise not to hold to that assumption. It may persuade the Council to provide a more secure basis for future planning based on a three year forward commitment. Even this recommendation, now being explored by the Minister for the Arts, would put Covent Garden in a privileged position vis-à-vis new artistic ventures. Through its purposeful retiring chairman, Sir Claus Moser, the Garden has taken these constraints on the Council as a sign that even more of its efforts should be directed at attracting private finance and at persuading the government to treat it as a special case.

Good luck to Sir Claus and his colleagues in seeking further funding from private sources, which could include a look at ticket pricing policy. The arguments for separate government funding, however, need careful examination. They amount to an attempt to convince us that Covent Garden Opera confers more uncovenanted benefits on us all per extra pound spent than would other cultural institutions.

The first supposed benefit can be easily dismissed – the idea that the existence of Covent Garden Opera is essential for the survival of regional opera. But regional companies have created audiences with distinct preference patterns; if they look anywhere for a lead, it is more likely to be towards the English National Opera.

The second claim is that the Garden is central to the conservation and development of our national culture. In recent years British composers have been in the van in the creation of new operatic ventures, and the Garden has promoted some of these. But even the most fanatical supporter of opera would subscribe to a long list of comparable cultural institutions which deserve support. Any consideration of public funding for the Garden must take account of the alternative cultural benefits forgone.

The third claim is that our international cultural prestige has replaced economic supremacy as a contributor towards our general satisfaction. The Garden could indeed count itself as one of the complex or metropolitan cultural institutions which supports this end, even if the principal singers, producers, designers and conductors come from abroad and mount mainly German, Italians, and Russian operas in the original language. This might make a case for some form of export subsidy but hardly one for a considerably larger production grant. The government might contract with the Garden to buy blocks of tickets (at commercial prices) which could then be distributed free to the international community through embassies, the British Council and the like. This is no more outlandish than the tax concessions for certain export goods granted to tourists. Accepting special funding for a small exclusive group of national companies would lead to the balkanisation of arts financing, a highly complicated bargaining structure between such companies and the government, and the consequent creation of a bureaucratic paradise.

A very respectable general case can be made for much more spending on the creative and performed arts, though coupled with more efficient and economical methods of funding. That case is not helped by attempting to create privileged artistic empires, immune from competitive tendering for public funding and from the judgment of their peers.

I had taken the precaution of sending the article in advance of publication to the ACGB Secretary-General but there was no reaction. I had made it clear – as the text shows – that I was following out the implications of ACGB policy which I fully supported. I knew that I was trailing my coat and expected some controversy and perhaps some of the things I said were too pointed. But I hardly expected the wrath to come. Perhaps the robustness of my controversies in 1986 with TV personalities who were upset by the findings of the Committee on Financing the BBC had made me forget how sensitive are the toes of the custodians of the higher culture.

Fortunately for me, those who viewed my criticism of the Garden's tactics as a sacrilegious utterance played it very badly. Their first ploy was to protest to William Rees-Mogg, then Chairman of the ACGB, in no uncertain terms, one of the protesters being a member of the Council who issued the terrible threat that he could no longer sit round the same table with me. William must have had difficulty in knowing what to do, and, inadvisedly I believe, admonished me by drawing attention to the rules governing public statements by members of the ACGB which, by my interpretation, had not been breached. His letter could be construed as containing the presumption of guilt before I had even had time to speak to him, and, recognising this, he generously agreed to my proposal that he withdraw his letter as I would my rather testy reply to him. I had cause to be grateful to him when Roy Strong without notice and without declaring his interest – his wife Julia Trevelyan being a member of the Covent Garden staff – demanded that the Chairman of the ACGB should disassociate himself from what I had said. William adopted the Voltairian stance of disagreeing with what I had to say but defending my right to say it, and quietly had the matter dropped. I am not proud of the letter that I sent to Roy Strong which began 'next time, dear boy, you wish to question my credentials, have the courtesy to give me notice and the temerity to declare your interest' – but I enjoyed writing it. His reply is not up to the high standard of discourse we expect from him so I shall not embarrass him by revealing its contents.

The final encounter before this storm in a largish teacup blew over was with none other than Wynne Godley, the Cambridge economist, whom I greatly admire. He had been appointed a Trustee of Covent Garden and could bring to the post not only his professional skills but also his experience as a one-time professional oboe player. He is not a man to write tongue-in-cheek but I was amazed to find him using a feeble *argumentum ad hominem* as a way of discrediting what I had said. In a letter to *The Times* on 1 April 1987 he construed my article as really being a pitch for more money for the arts in Scotland! I was able to reply that I was on public record as having said that the SAC had received its due in the annual financial carve-up but that it was not without interest perhaps that the annual grant to Covent Garden Opera and Ballet was almost exactly equal to the annual sum that the SAC received to cover funding of the arts in all Scotland! Such are the advantages of incumbency, but if anyone had at that time a complaint about inequitable funding, it was the English regions and not Scotland.

I have no illusions about the lack of impact of attempts to bring some element of consistency into arts funding, and Covent Garden is a good example of an institution which is in a strong position to pull out the emotional stops and envelop London-bound politicians and their advisers in an orgy of sound which could soften their hearts along with their brains. No wonder that successive Ministers for the Arts and Chairmen of the ACGB, as decently as possible, have obfuscated the connection between policy and practice so that opera does not appear to have been unduly favoured in the funding stakes. Perhaps the protests about favouring the art-form so cherished by the relatively rich will be stilled by the impact of 'circus opera' on Pavarottian lines and of Classic FM Radio on the popular mind. The day may come when a million signatures could easily be found to sign a petition demanding that Covent Garden should have first cut on the proceeds of the National Lottery.

LA COMMEDIA È FINITA

The Prisoner of Chillon in Byron's once-famous poem 'regained his freedom with a sigh'.

There are certainly things to be missed in holding public office but it is storing up trouble for oneself if one muses too much over what one did and what one might have done. The record, such as it is, is there and others, if anyone is interested, can make their own judgments. There is no temptation to offer a homily on my experiences, and I have preferred to introduce general observations throughout this book, when events suggested them. The best short statement about the difficulties and distresses of holding public office that I have ever come across saves me the embarrassment of an epilogue. It was written by William Wildman – hardly an indication of his nature – Viscount Barrington who was the Secretary at War in the reign of George III for no less than nineteen years, the modern equivalent of a Permanent Secretary. In that capacity he had to cope with every conceivable kind of demand and plea from the armies in the field and from influential families trying to place their sons in commissioned employment. In an official letter to the Judge Advocate-General, one of his senior colleagues, he wrote as follows:

> [T]he Officer of the Crown who is entrusted with the charge of the whole Army, a Body whose probable duration infinitely exceeds the short Space allotted to Individuals, cannot be too vigilant, lest confin'd temporary convenience or Compassion, should produce general permanent mischief or distress. To be firm in preventing future evil by immediate refusal, is not the least difficult part of his Duty: He must withstand the feelings of humanity and the desire to please; he must expect the uncandid interpretation of the prejudic'd, the hasty judgment of the ignorant, and the malignant conclusion of the disappointed; Arrows shot in the Dark, against which a good conscience is an insufficient defence: He must often contradict the passions & Interests of the powerful; and even disappoint the wishes and expectations of the deserving: He must acquire a great many Enemies, and lose a great many friends; and yet he had better suffer all this than do wrong. (Hayter, 1988, pp. 298–9)

8

FINALE
The Economist and the Musician

D ennis Robertson – in his day almost as famous as Keynes – observed at a meeting of the British Association for the Advancement of Science many years ago that, whatever disadvantage economists faced in conducting empirical investigation, they could at least sit down and have dinner with their subject matter, which he was in the process of doing! Certainly, if your investigations require the co-operation of your subject matter, then there is much to be said for developing a relationship where they can come to know and trust you. Then you may be given not only the information you desire but also a frank assessment of its quality and are more likely to be made aware of the traps for the unwary in making inferences from data about individual and collective behaviour in the economic activity in question. But a warning is necessary, which I have never been able to heed completely. It is a well-known phenomenon in social investigation that the investigator risks being captured by his subject matter. Anthropologists have been known to begin investigation of the mores of distant tribes as *soi-disant* impartial observers and to finish up fully identifying themselves with their rituals, customs and aspirations. The process can go further with potentially embarrassing results when the 'scientists' become committed advocates of the political aspirations of tribes often implacably opposed to the policy of their governments. I have often wondered whether I was not undergoing the same experience having in the course of my enquiries met so many creative and performing artists whose talents I appreciated all the more from being all too well aware of a skill and dedication to their art which I could never possess. Perhaps then Tibor Scitovsky was right, and here was a dilemma which 'cultural economists' in particular have to face, and which they may never be able to resolve. Whether or not my 'capture' by the music profession is complete I do not think that it has distorted my judgment sufficiently to make my analysis suspect to economists and musicians alike. Readers must judge for themselves, but before passing judgment, perhaps a few remarks of justification of my claim will help.

One of the abortive pieces of research conducted for the orchestral enquiry (see Chapter 4) was a survey of the attitudes of music students at York towards orchestral performance as a profession. The results were unusable mainly because John Lazarus and I had not done enough 'softening up' to allay any suspicions about the motive for the enquiry, so that the response rate was low. What can be said is that students in general had very little idea about the realities of life after graduation which, if they continued as musicians, meant that they would be performers or teachers rather than composers and musicologists. Moreover, a fair proportion of them clearly believed that they should be spared the trauma of making a living from satisfying audiences or pupils and should receive continuing and lasting state support to allow them the time and leisure to think great thoughts and to write masterpieces with long gestation periods.

I began this book by remarking how one's life is often punctuated by the failure of being able to live up to one's own perceptions of what one seeks from it and what one feels capable of achieving. I added that this need not make one feel bitter and twisted. I wonder, nevertheless, whether our aspirant composers and performers and, indeed, budding creative artists in general, are not more vulnerable to this kind of disappointment, and more affected by them, given the particular risks that they face and the lack of warning. I know that things have changed quite radically in music schools and that several of them have courses designed for students who hope to specialise in community work of some kind. This introduces them at an early stage to the challenges of turning their knowledge and skills to practical use. At the same time, there is also a case for not propelling students too quickly in the direction of the harsh realities of earning a living before they have acquired the intellectual capital and maturity which enables them to face the future. I don't expect music schools to provide courses in the political economy of music, but career advice should offer something more than immediate job prospects, limited though these may be, and should include some kind of perspectives about the organisation of the profession and its relation with those who provide its remuneration. Perhaps my attempts to understand musicians and to help them in turn to understand the attitudes of those who benefit from their services suggest how those entering the profession might be better informed.

The musicians at the sharp end of the 'trade' may be unimpressed. As I have repeatedly emphasised, either as individual soloists, singers or instrumentalists, or as collective entities such as orchestras or opera companies, they have learnt through bitter experience how to protect their interests. One interesting facet of the organisation of musical performance has been the close involvement of players in the governance of their companies, both in the labour-managed London orchestras and in the gradual concession of places on boards of management where players are employees. I do not believe that one can generalise about the optimal ownership and management structure of opera, music theatre and orchestral companies, but surely it is beyond question that being in a position to understand the constraints under which management has to operate in running a successful company requires a close association of musicians with its major decisions. If there is one thing that those working musicians must have learnt through such experience, it is that governments cannot be relied on to remove the major economic uncertainties which confront them. Put round the other way, the necessary condition for continuing in business must be the satisfaction of the final buyer – the public at large.

Nor is there any reason to suppose that the situation will alter simply because bodies such as the Arts Councils perceive their role to be not only that of allocating funds but of advocating that the arts are underfunded, which is the persistent message in recent documents such as the Charter for the Arts (ACGB, forthcoming) and its Scots counterpart The Charter for the Arts in Scotland. As I advocated at the time of their preparation, such documents are useless unless the proposals are costed, as, I may say, were the proposals of the Orchestral Enquiry (see Chapter 4).

There are two tactical reasons why costings are avoided apart from the work involved in producing reasonable estimates. The first is that invidious comparisons would have to be revealed between different art-forms as reflected in the sums allocated to each. One can imagine the disputes which might arise if the artistic judgment of the ACGB implied in the estimates that, for example, less resources should be devoted to support of symphony orchestras and more towards development of appreciation of modern painting. The second is that the sponsors of such exercises could fall victim to their own honesty. However qualified such estimates may be and however carefully presented and commented on, they can too easily become the source of deliberate misunderstanding amongst those who are opposed to the whole idea of any form of government involvement at any level in the provision of finance for cultural activities. Yet at the end of the day, alongside the persuasive advocacy of the kind found in Roy Shaw's *The Arts and the People* (1987) – a book which I much admire though I reject his main arguments – resource costs have to be estimated and justified. If the exercise is not done by those who claim to know what government 'ought' to spend, then it will be done for them by the Treasury, which, in the light of competing claims for resources, will, of necessity, take a hard line.

If there is any message from my own experience, it is to advise musicians not to 'put their trust in princes'. They may have no alternative in the course of their education when it is largely state-provided and mainly financed by the taxpayer. But when it comes to making a living, rather than rely on deliverance from any government of whatever complexion or level, including the EC, to support them through the same generosity with taxpayers' money as the Berlin Philarmonic Orchestra enjoys, they would be better advised to plan on the assumption that they face the same uncertainties as others do who are not dependent on government for their salaries and wages or for their custom. I am not arguing that, as a point of principle, an orchestra or opera company should ostentatiously refuse to accept public money on offer, but it should be taken as a mark of excellence that, subject to the judgment of their peers which they respect, it manages to satisfy both artistic standards and the paying public. For too long, to be a charitable non-profit making corporation with 'National' or

'Royal' in its title and in receipt of a large government subsidy, has been taken to be the epitome of professional respectability.

I realise the dilemma which would confront orchestral and operatic managements who sought to follow this advice, and who believed that their high standards and artistic inclinations required them to face the challenge of promoting new works as well as offering conductors of orchestras or opera producers the opportunity of offering new interpretations of the standard repertoire. In this respect, as my narrative has emphasised at various points, they can only expect limited co-operation from composers. The day is probably too far away when the standard orchestral concert will consist of contemporary works with some past masterpiece as the esoteric item on the programme.

It is not being suggested that composers should make artistic compromises in order to satisfy managements worried about the effect of including X's Sinfonietta for gamelan, factory hooter, ondes martenot and strings (played col legno), which lasts for forty-five minutes, in their Summer Proms programme. There are other vehicles by which they can exploit their skills in order to make a living as a composer, such as TV and film background music. ('Twelve-tone Liz' – Elisabeth Lutyens to the uninitiated – claimed to be proud of her film music.) A very uneasy situation is bound to develop between orchestral managers and guilds of composers. Government-subsidised orchestras will be expected to promote contemporary music as a condition of receiving grants, but their managements are uncertain about the 'downside risk' where the dilemma is whether to face the loss of the grant by dodging the contemporary music requirement or the loss of audiences untutored in the finer points of post-serialist composition. The only answer, short of consigning contemporary music to the cultural ghettos created by small ensembles with a devoted following (which includes myself), is to target that part of their audience, inevitably a small minority, who would be willing to pay over the odds because they derive satisfaction from supporting the new and experimental. The enterprising English National Opera have had a manifest success in seeking extra-box-office support from opera-goers for special productions. I received, the morning of writing these words, a persuasive appeal to support a commission for a new composition to be played by a local chamber orchestra. Obviously, I applaud this approach for it fits with my view that the mark of excellence should be seen to be self-help without artistic compromise.

Understandably, there are composers who reject the view that there should be any sort of trade-off between public acceptability of a work and what they perceive to be the artistic criteria laid down by their peer group. Milton Babbitt has said (1966) that the 'top-class' composers are rather like research physicists and should therefore be judged by their contribution to new developments in compositional method rather than by the application of their professional skills. There is an exact parallel here in economics. Peer group assessment would identify as the top economists almost exclusively academics who have added a new twist to often very complicated economics models or who have invented a new conceptual framework for some part or even the whole of their discipline. Nobel prizes and membership of national academies, judged by prestigious committees of professors, are not awarded to those who have merely concentrated on making a manifest commercial success in selling their ideas to the public, though there are those who have had it both ways. Indeed, the publicity attached to such awards may increase the public demand for the services of those recognised by their fellows as their intellectual leaders. Long may this remain so, but always provided that composers and academic economists whose distinction has been buttressed by state support can convince those who finance them that they (or their heirs) will receive massive unconvenanted benefits from efforts to extend the frontiers of knowledge.

The dialogue between the musician and the economist which I have illustrated in this book is not carried out purely with a view to seeking parallels of approach to learning which would lead to mutual respect amongst scholars. A neglected branch of economics concerns the devising of ways of adapting institutions so that they offer a better delivery of the services that they are meant to perform. Of course, as is evident from my narrative, the perceived need for adaptation depends on one's personal view of cultural objectives and one's view may be one of many. Nor is there any guarantee that if objectives were agreed, this would point towards only one method for attaining them or agreement about the ranking of the likely success of the alternative institutional changes that might be necessary. Thus even if all agreed with Keynes's vision of a world in which increases in living standards would be accompanied by a more than proportionate increase in individuals' demand for cultural pursuits, there is strong disagreement about both the desirability and feasibility of using government action to move in Keynes's direction. I have tried to show how economic analysis can be used to achieve some degree of consistency in ends and means, using policies which have affected music as my main example. In doing so, one is bound to be critical of the woolly reasoning which often pervades thinking about 'paying the piper' and the consequential tendency to use a smokescreen of words to disguise the lack of cohesion in cultural policy. An economist who simply wanted to improve or maintain his professional standing might, nowadays at least, do so by using modelling and statistical skills to examine the activities of those who conduct and are affected by cultural policies. He would then seek publication in the better professional journals, garnishing his analysis with perhaps some pithy quotations from, say, Benvenuto Cellini's memoirs or Schoenberg's correspondence to lighten the task of the reader. There is no harm in this – I must admit to having employed this strategy – but this is not a recipe for improving credibility if the aim is to interest and to influence those who are the subject of his/her investigation. To achieve the status of being heard in the debate on cultural policies entails a commitment to working one's passage with professional creative and performing artists through the difficult task of explaining simple but strangely unfamiliar economic propositions. This task was made much easier for me than it might have been by the fact that, as musicians would put it, I was (unexpectedly) offered engagements and did not have to seek promotions! I hope that those who follow me into the field of cultural economics will be made equally welcome by those whose activities they study, and, for their part, appreciate the opportunity to throw light on the workings of an ancient and honourable profession – and have as much fun as I did!

BIBLIOGRAPHY

(As well as cited works, the bibliography includes several references which have been useful to the author, and may be equally useful to the reader.)

ARTS COUNCIL OF GREAT BRITAIN (1967) *Twenty-Second Annual Report* for year ended 31 March 1967.

ARTS COUNCIL OF GREAT BRITAIN (1970) *A Report on Orchestral Resources in Great Britain* ('Peacock' Report).

ARTS COUNCIL OF GREAT BRITAIN (1992) *Forty-Seventh Annual Report* for year ended 31 March 1992.

ARTS COUNCIL OF GREAT BRITAIN (forthcoming) *The Charter for the Arts.*

ASSOCIATION OF PROFESSIONAL COMPOSERS (1989) *The Electric-Composer Commissioning Guidelines*, APC Publishing, London.

BABBITT, MILTON (1966) 'Who Cares if you Listen?', in CHASE, GILBERT (ed.) *The American Composer Speaks*, Lousiana State University Press.

BAUMOL, HILDA and BAUMOL, WILLIAM J. (eds) (1984) *Inflation and The Performing Arts*, New York University Press.

BAUMOL, WILLIAM J. and BOWEN, WILLIAM G. (1966) *The Performing Arts: The Economic Dilemma*, Twentieth Century Fund.

BLAUG, M. (ed.) (1976), *The Economics of the Arts*, Martin Robertson, London.

DART, THURSTON (1954) *The Interpretation of Music*, Hutchinson's University Library.

DART, THURSTON (1965) 'Musical Dinosaurs and Operational Research', *Musical Times*, August.

EAST, LESLIE (1980) 'Wilfrid (Howard) Mellers', in SADIE, STANLEY (ed.) *The New Grove Dictionary of Music and Musicians*, Macmillan, London, Vol. 12, pp. 108–10.

EHRLICH, CYRIL (1989) *Harmonious Alliance: a History of the Performing Right Society*, Oxford University Press, Oxford.

EISLER, HANNS (1964) *Sinn und Form, Sonderheft fur Hanns Eisler*, Rutter und Loening, Berlin.

FEIST, A. W. and HUTCHINSON R. (1990) *Funding the Arts in Seven Western Countries: Cultural Trends, 1990*, Policy Studies Institute, London.

FREY, B. S. and POMMEREHNE, W. W. (1989) *Muses and Markets: Explorations in the Economics of the Arts*, Basil Blackwell, Oxford.

FULLERTON, D. (1991) 'On Public Justifications for Public Support of the Arts', *Journal of Cultural Economics*, Vol. 15, No. 2., December.

GAL, HANS (1965) *The Musician's World*, Thames and Hudson, London.

GLASGOW, MARY (1975) 'The Concept of the Arts Council', in KEYNES, MILO (ed.) *Essays on John Maynard Keynes*, Cambridge University Press.

GOODMAN, ARNOLD (LORD GOODMAN) *et al.* (1965) *Report of the Committee on the London Orchestras*, HMSO, London..

GRAY, CECIL (1987) *Musical Chairs*, The Hogarth Press, London.

HARRIES, MEIRION and HARRIES, SUSIE (1989) *A Pilgrim Soul: The Life and Work of Elizabeth Lutyens*, Faber and Faber, London.

HAYTER, TONY (ed.) (1988) *An Eighteenth-Century Secretary at War: The Papers of William, Viscount Barrington*, The Bodley Head for the Army Records Society.

HIGGINS, JOHN (1965) *Public Patronage and the Arts*, PEP.

HINDEMITH, PAUL (1953) *A Composer's World*, Harvard.

HMSO (1977) *Copyright and Design Laws* (Cmnd. Paper No. 6732) ('Whitford' Report).

HMSO (1986) *Intellectual Property and Innovation* (Cmnd. Paper No. 9712).

HMSO (1993) *The Charter for the Arts in Scotland*, Edinburgh.

HOME OFFICE (1986) *Report of the Committee on Financing the BBC* (Peacock Report), Cmnd. Paper No. 9824, HMSO, London.

HONEGGER, ARTHUR (1966) *I am a Composer*, St Martin's Press, New York.

KING, K. and BLAUG, M. (1973) 'Does the Arts Council Know What It is Doing?', *Encounter*, September, reproduced in BLAUG (1976).

LAMBERT, CONSTANT (1948) *Music Ho!*, Pelican, London.

LANDON, H. C. ROBBINS (1980) *Haydn: The Early Years 1732–1765*, Thames and Hudson, London.

LANDON, H. C. ROBBINS (1988) *Mozart's Last Year, 1791*, Thames and Hudson, London.

LANDON, H. C. ROBBINS (1989) *Mozart, The Golden Years 1781–1791*, Thames and Hudson, London.

LARNER, GERALD (1980) 'David Blake', in *The New Grove Dictionary of Music and Musicians*, Macmillan, London, Vol. 2, p. 775.

MASON, D. (1987) *Expounding the Arts*, Adam Smith Institute, London.

MOSER, CLAUS (1981) Evidence to the Education, Science and Arts Committee, House of Commons, 29 June.

MYERSCOUGH, J. (1988) *The Economic Importance of the Arts in Britain*, Policy Studies Institute, London.

PEACOCK, ALAN (1969) 'Welfare Economics and Public Subsidies to the Arts', reproduced in BLAUG, (1976).

PEACOCK, ALAN (1976) 'The "Output" of the London Orchestras 1966–75', *Musical Times*, August.

PEACOCK, ALAN (1979) 'Public Policy and Copyright in Music', in *The Economic Analysis of Government*, Martin Robertson, London.

PEACOCK, ALAN (1987) 'Pruning the Garden', *The Times*, 14 March.

PEACOCK, ALAN (1992) 'Economics, Cultural Values and Cultural Policies', in TOWSE, R. and KHAKEE, A. (eds) *Cultural Economics*, Springer-Verlag, Berlin.

PEACOCK, ALAN and GODFREY, C. (1973) 'Cultural Accounting', *Social Trends*, November, reproduced in BLAUG (1976).

PEACOCK, ALAN and WEIR, RONALD (1975) *The Composer in the Market Place*, Faber Music Ltd, London.

PEACOCK, ALAN, SHOESMITH, E. and MILNER, G. (1983) *Inflation and the Performed Arts*, Arts Council of Great Britain, London.

PERFORMING RIGHT SOCIETY LTD (1989) *Yearbook 1989–90*, London.

PERFORMING RIGHT SOCIETY LTD (1990a) *Yearbook 1990–91*, London.

PERFORMING RIGHT SOCIETY LTD (1990b) *PRS News*, No. 31, Autumn.

REED, JOHN (1972) *Schubert: The Final Years*, Faber and Faber, London.

ROBBINS, L. C. (1971) 'Unsettled Questions in the Political Economy of the Arts', reproduced in BLAUG (1976).

ROCKEFELLER PANEL (1965) *The Performing Arts: Problems and Prospects*, McGraw Hill, New York.

ROTH, ERNST (1969) *The Business of Music*, Cassell, London.

RUMP, ALAN (1977) *Money for Composers*, Arts Council of Great Britain.

SCHAFER, R. MURRAY (1965) *The Composer in the Classroom*, Berandol Music Ltd, Toronto.

SCHOENBERG, ARNOLD, Letter to von Zemlinsky, reproduced in GAL, HANS (ed.) *The Musician's World*, Thames and Hudson, London, 1965, p 441.

SCITOVSKY, T. (1972) 'What's Wrong with the Arts is What's Wrong with Society', *American Economic Review* reproduced in BLAUG (1976).

SCITOVSKY, T. (1983) 'Subsidies for the Arts: The Economic Argument', in HENDON, W. S. and SHANAHAN, J. L. (eds) *Economics of Cultural Decisions*, Abt Books, Cambridge, Mass.

SHAW, BERNARD (1955) *Shaw on Music*, Doubleday and Co.

SHAW, ROY (1987) *The Arts and the People*, Cape, London.

SHUBIK, M. (1985) *A Game-Theoretic Approach to Political Economy*, The MIT Press, Cambridge, Mass.

SMITH, ADAM (1776) *An Inquiry into the Nature and Causes of the Wealth of Nations* (ed. by R. H. CAMPBELL and A. S. SKINNER), Clarendon Press, Oxford, 1976.

STIGLER, GEORGE (1991) 'The Direction of Economic Research' in SHAW, G. K. (ed.) *Economics, Culture and Education: Essays in Honour of Mark Blaug*, Edward Elgar, Aldershot.

STRAVINSKY, IGOR (1962) *Stravinsky in Conversation with Robert Craft*, Penguin Books.

THOMSON, VIRGIL (1962) *The State of Music* (second edition, revised), Vintage Books, New York

THROSBY, C. D. and WITHERS, G. A. (1979) *The Economics of the Performing Arts*, Edward Arnold, London.

TIPPETT, MICHAEL (1959) *Moving into Aquarius*, Routledge and Kegan Paul, London.

TOWSE, RUTH (1993) *Singers in the Marketplace*, Clarendon Press, Oxford.

WEST, E. G. (1985) *Subsidizing the Performing Arts*, Ontario Economic Council: Policy Study Series, Toronto.

WILSON, CONRAD (1980) 'Hans Gal', in SADIE, STANLEY (ed.) *The New Grove Dictionary of Music and Musicians*, Macmillan, London, Vol. 7, pp. 90–1.

WITHERS, G. (1985) 'Artists' Subsidy of the Arts' in WAITS C. R., HENDON W. S. and HUROVITZ, H. (ed.), *Governments and Cultures*, Association for Cultural Economics, University of Akron, Ohio.

INDEX OF NAMES